Twayne's United States Authors Series

Warren French
Editor

W. D. Snodgrass

TUSAS 316

W. D. SNODGRASS

By PAUL L. GASTON

Southern Illinois University

TWAYNE PUBLISHERS

A DIVISION OF G. K. HALL & CO., BOSTON

Copyright © 1978 by G. K. Hall & Co.

Published in 1978 by Twayne Publishers,
A Division of G. K. Hall & Co.
All Rights Reserved

Printed on permanent/durable acid-free paper and bound
in the United States of America

First Printing

Library of Congress Cataloging in Publication Data

Gaston, Paul.
W. D. Snodgrass.

(Twayne's United States authors series ; TUSAS 316)
Bibliography: p. 167 - 70
Includes index.
1.   Snodgrass, William De Witt, 1926 -
—Criticism and interpretation.
PS3537.N32Z6   811'.5'4   78-5477
ISBN 0-8057-7242-1

For Elizabeth

Contents

About the Author

Paul L. Gaston, who received both graduate degrees from the University of Virginia, is now Associate Professor of English at Southern Illinois University, Edwardsville. Since taking the Ph.D. in 1970, Mr. Gaston has been the recipient of three grants from the National Endowment for the Humanities and has published articles on Walker Percy, Ben Jonson, interart analogies, and Joseph Conrad, as well as on W. D. Snodgrass. He has been appointed volume editor for *The Arrow of Gold* in the forthcoming edition by the Cambridge University Press of The Complete Works of Joseph Conrad. In addition to courses in sixteenth- and twentieth-century literature, Mr. Gaston teaches courses in writing, in song, and in the Bible.

Preface

If quantity of production were a measure of distinction, W. D. Snodgrass would have to be considered a minor poet. In the quarter-century of his career, Snodgrass has published only three volumes of poetry under his own name, two books of translations, and one collection of critical essays. Even if we include the few poems that have not yet been published in a collection, we are likely to think the body of Snodgrass's work small for a poet so influential and widely admired.

We do not, however, measure poets like we measure corn. That we can read and understand the works of a poet in a single evening is no criticism if the evening becomes a highly challenging and rewarding one.

I do not make the same claim for an evening spent with this brief introductory study. It is a means to an end—the enjoyment of Snodgrass's poems—and it should be read in conjunction with at least *Heart's Needle, After Experience,* and *The Führer Bunker.* Accordingly, rather than espouse a controlling critical thesis, I attempt to encourage and assist in the close reading of a substantial part of Snodgrass's work. I was once given a set of study scores for the symphonies of Beethoven; in each score, carefully placed arrows indicate the introduction of principal and subordinate subjects, point to the ways in which they are developed, and designate the patterns into which their development falls. I hope that my analyses of Snodgrass's poems provide much the same kind of assistance without being much more obtrusive.

To this end, I have tried to supply assistance where it seems most needed and to give considerably less attention to matters which seem to require little explanation.

In Chapter One, for instance, I offer a short characterization of the poetry of contemporary personal experience, popularly known as "confessional" poetry, together with a preliminary examination of four experiences of Snodgrass's life that have proved particularly important as conditions and as subjects for his poetry. But I do not provide even a small-scale traditional biography. Any reader can observe the most pertinent dates and events in Snodgrass's life by reviewing the chronology included here, and Snodgrass himself provides in his early poems the most revealing treatment of those biographical episodes crucial to him and to his art.

Chapters Two and Three, which cover *Heart's Needle*, and Chapters Five and Six, which cover most of *After Experience*, are longer and more detailed, for they offer analyses of poems with which the reader is most likely to want assistance. Chapter Six, which discusses Snodgrass's five poems on modern paintings, is particularly detailed, because an approach to these complex and important works requires some knowledge of the paintings as well as close attention to complex poetic strategies.

Chapter Four provides efficient summaries of poems in *Remains*, a pseudonymous 1970 collection, and limited critical analyses of them. Although some of the poems collected in *Remains* first appeared in literary periodicals, the collection itself was published in an edition of only two hundred copies, most of which made their way at once to rare book collections. Anyone interested in Snodgrass's poetry should know what these poems say, but detailed explication of poems that many readers will be able to obtain only with difficulty would hardly suit the purposes of an introductory study.

Chapter Seven provides a preliminary discussion of the recently published *The Führer Bunker*, one based in large part on an extensive interview with the poet. Because this study is concerned with an active poet, it seems appropriate that the final substantial chapter should provide at least an indirect means by which the poet is able to communicate with his potential readers. And any attempt on my part at definitive evaluation of a work still "in progress" would be premature.

Chapter Eight, an afterword, attempts to provide an additional perspective on Snodgrass's continuing growth by concentrating briefly on his translations and criticism. In a more highly specialized study, both would deserve far more attention. Obviously, there can be no "conclusion," as such, for an introduction to the works of a poet in the midst of his career.

I can conclude this preface, though, and want to do so by acknowledging assistance I have received. Southern Illinois University granted me a six month sabbatical leave, during which I was able to begin my research and writing. John Irvine Ades, Daniel Havens, and Betty Richardson, as successive chairpersons of the department of English, and Dale Bailey and Carol Keene, as successive deans of the school of humanities, have provided encouragement and assistance. The staffs of Lovejoy Library at Southern Illinois University, of Firestone Library at Princeton University, of Mugar Memorial Library at Boston University, and of the Romanian Library, New York, have been cordial and helpful.

I owe special thanks to Mr. Snodgrass for his hospitality and generous assistance.

Jeanne Bailey typed the manuscript with unusual care, efficiency, and cheerfulness. Warren French made many valuable suggestions for its improvement. William White provided useful bibliographical information. Eileen Gaston, my wife, has helped with proofreading at every stage; she has a sharp eye for errors and a soft voice in which to report them, and I thank her for both.

Acknowledgments

Quotations from *Heart's Needle*, by W. D. Snodgrass, copyright ©1959 by William Snodgrass, are reprinted by permission of Alfred A. Knopf, Inc., and by permission of The Marvel Press.

Quotations from *After Experience*, by W. D. Snodgrass, copyright ©1968 by W. D. Snodgrass, are reprinted by permission of Harper & Row, Publishers, Inc.

Quotations from *Remains*, by S. S. Gardons, copyright © 1969 by W. D. Snodgrass, are reprinted by permission of the author.

Quotations from *The Fuhrer Bunker: A Cycle of Poems in Progress*, by W. D. Snodgrass, copyright ©1977 by W. D. Snodgrass, are reprinted by permission of BOA Editions.

Chronology

1926   January 5: William DeWitt Snodgrass born in Wilkinsburg, Pennsylvania.

1943   Begins undergraduate studies at Geneva College, Beaver Falls, Pennsylvania.

1944   Drafted into U.S. Navy; serves on Saipan in Pacific.

1946   Resumes undergraduate studies at Geneva College; marries Lila Jean Hank; transfers to University of Iowa.

1949   Receives B.A. from University of Iowa.

1951   Receives M.A. from University of Iowa.

1953   Divorced from Lila Jean Hank; receives M.F.A. from University of Iowa.

1954   Marries Janice Marie Ferguson Wilson.

1955   Leader of Poetry Workshop, Morehead Writers' Conference; appointed instructor in English, Cornell University.

1957   Appointed instructor in English, University of Rochester.

1958   Poet in residence, Antioch Writers' Conference; receives Ingram Merrill Foundation Award; receives *Hudson Review* fellowship in poetry.

1959   Appointed assistant professor in English, Wayne State University, Detroit; publishes *Heart's Needle*; receives Longview Foundation Literary Award.

1960   Receives citation from Poetry Society of America, grant from the National Institute of Arts and Letters, and Pulitzer Prize for poetry.

1961   Receives Guinness Poetry Award (Great Britain).

1963   Receives grant from Ford Foundation.

1966   Receives Miles Poetry Award; divorced from Janice Marie Ferguson Wilson.

1967   Publishes translation of *Gallows Songs* by Christian Morgenstern, in collaboration with Lore Segal; marries Camille Rykowski.

1968   Appointed professor in English and Speech, Syracuse University; publishes *After Experience*.

1970 "S. S. Gardons" publishes *Remains*.

1972 Named Guggenheim Fellow; named member of National Institute of Arts and Letters.

1973 Receives Academy of American Poets fellowship.

1975 Publishes *In Radical Pursuit;* collaborates with Ioan A. Popa on English translation of *Miorita*, published in multilingual edition in Cluj, Romania.

1976 Awarded Order of Cultural Merit (Second Class) by Romania; awarded Bicentennial medal, The College of William and Mary.

1977 Publishes *The Führer Bunker* and *Six Troubadour Songs* (translations).

1978 Writer in residence (spring semester), Old Dominion University, Norfolk, Virginia.

CHAPTER 1

Snodgrass and the Poetry of Contemporary Experience

IN 1959, W. D. Snodgrass published his first collection of poetry, *Heart's Needle*. Widely praised for both its craftsmanship and its candor, it offered its early readers the fresh voice of a young poet intent on examining his experience, learning about himself, and writing about the things he cared about most. So highly personal are the poems in the volume that the poet's grand proclamation of his own name in one of them, "These Trees Stand . . ," seems not at all inappropriate. Meditating upon himself as he wanders the woods on a dark night, weighing his capabilities, his limitations, his recovered pleasure in the world outside himself, he asserts, "Snodgrass is walking through the universe."

The strength of such poetry has been measured, both by its critics and by Snodgrass himself, in terms of "the depth of its sincerity," for it attempts to establish, in the poet's own words, "the only reality which a man can ever surely know . . . that self he cannot help being."[1] *Heart's Needle* is, among other things, a chronicle of the poet's attempt to understand himself and his private actions, as well as a disclosure of truths uncovered in the attempt.

But the poetry of *Heart's Needle*, which remains Snodgrass's best known achievement, represents an early and distinct stage of his still developing career. A few other poems on highly personal subjects appear in the first part of *After Experience* (1968), but Snodgrass's more recent poetry is clear evidence of his unwillingness to write "that kind of very personal poem . . . anymore."[2]

In many of the poems of *After Experience*, as in most of those that have come afterwards, the persistent concerns are neither intimate nor domestic, but social, philosophical, and historical. Style changes accordingly. Snodgrass developed complex and highly demanding forms for his poems on highly personal subjects, and he

15

cast them in straightforward, natural language. But his more recent poems tend to appear in free, experimental forms, and their language to a far greater extent calls attention to itself.

One good example of the widening range of subject and style in Snodgrass's poetry is the title poem of *After Experience*, which juxtaposes the voice of a combat instructor with that of the Dutch philosopher, Spinoza, in order to sustain a moral, philosophical challenge. Another such example is "An Elm Tree." As in "These Trees Stand. . . . ," the poet regards the woods. Instead of looking within himself in order to proclaim his name, however, he looks beyond himself and finds his name in the world. In the coldest part of the winter, he listens to birds darting through his trees: "One of them knows my name: / Chick-a-dee-dee-dee-dee-dee."[3]

The most dramatic indication of Snodgrass's ability to grow in unexpected directions lies in a complex, innovative collection, *The Führer Bunker* (1977), which Snodgrass has published as a work "in progress." If we discover in Snodgrass's earlier collections a gradual progression toward an increasingly objective view of the world, we can find a fruition of that progression in *The Führer Bunker*. From poems of the personal life, Snodgrass seems to have come at last to a poem entirely in the world. Yet, as we shall find in Chapter Seven, this poem, an extended study of Hitler's final days, is paradoxically highly personal as well. *The Führer Bunker* revives the crucial issues of *Heart's Needle* and subjects them to further analysis.

To be sure, Snodgrass continues to write the poetry of experience, but his experience now includes this reconstruction of Hitler's last days, the imaginative analysis of modern paintings, and Frost-like regret for man's insensitivity to nature, as in a poem titled "Cherry Saplings."[4] And the balance of honesty and craftsmanship that distinguishes his early poems is still present, though the means by which it is maintained are largely different ones.

I   *Snodgrass and "Confessional" Poetry*

Snodgrass has never thought "confessional" an especially accurate or felicitous adjective for his poetry on highly personal subjects, nor has he ever regarded himself as a founding member of a "school" so designated. Moreover, nearly two decades have passed since the publication of *Heart's Needle*, and Snodgrass does not write "that kind of very personal poem" anymore. Yet, the strong influence of Snodgrass's first collection remains manifest, and the term "confessional" seems to have won general acceptance. The questions that matter are these: Is the contemporary poetry we call "confessional" and attribute to poets like Snodgrass, Robert Lowell, Sylvia Plath, and Anne Sexton in any way different from earlier first-person poems on private subjects? And, if so, what particular contribution has Snodgrass made to this new "tradition"?

At the height of the popularity of "confessional" poetry, it became fashionable to remind readers that such poetry was not, in fact, anything new. "There have always been 'confessional' poets," John Lehmann told an interviewer, citing Shakespeare's sonnets as his proof. "If they make good poetry out of their confessions, I am all for it."[5] Up to a point, the remark is instructive. There is a long tradition of poetry in which the primary intent seems neither dramatic nor descriptive, but self-revealing, and many of those who have contributed to it, from Shakespeare and George Herbert through the Romantics to Whitman and Frost, have given us suggestive analogues for modern poems of the self. And an even longer tradition, that of song, further illustrates the antiquity of the impulses we now may call "confessional." Indeed, if all that we mean by the term is the application of the "I" voice to personal subjects, Lehmann is entirely correct, and the efforts of such poets as Snodgrass and Lowell are but another outcropping of a vein never far beneath the surface.

It is precisely awareness of the early analogues to the "confessional" poetry of the 1950s and 1960s, however, which makes it possible for us to discern that such poetry does represent a fresh initiative within its broad tradition; that, in short, Snodgrass and Lowell and those influenced by them are poets whose achievement is in several respects unusual. While it is commendable to be "all for" the confessional tradition in its broadest terms, and while it is useful to appreciate its longevity, it is not less important to try to define those qualities that distinguish the contemporary manifestation of the confessional mode.

One obvious but significant quality of the poetry we regard as confessional is its high degree of specialization in the revelation of the poet's private concerns. The contemporary confessional poet is regarded as such not because he or she writes some poems that may be considered confessional, but because he or she has organized the confessional impulse into discrete and consistent projections of his or her personality. It follows that the poetry we discuss as confessional has characteristically attracted our attention as sequences,

or volumes, or sequences of volumes. Poets like James Dickey and
Mark Strand have published good poems with emphases we might
describe as confessional, but because they have done so irregularly,
in careers notable for diversity and versatility, we tend not to
associate them with the confessional poets.

And with good reason. The distinction is more significant than it
may seem, for it can remind us that the poets we consider confessional seem to have devoted themselves exclusively during a
given period of time to the hard demands of the confessional form.
Indeed, some seem to have been consumed by the confessional impulse. Lowell and Snodgrass both have spoken with relief of having
moved out of it. The point is that confessional poetry, as we know it
in the works of Plath and Sexton and Lowell and Snodgrass, seems
not a genre close at hand for occasional adoption, but the only
plausible stylistic alternative appropriate to a specific period of
acute psychological and artistic introspection.

One important result of this tendency toward specialization is
that collections of confessional poetry not only reflect upon the
character of the poet-speaker, but also, poem by poem, constitute it
for the reader. When we read Snodgrass's "A Cardinal," as we shall
see, we can take some grave amusement in observing the poet's
projecting his preoccupations onto the innocent songbird, but we
may at the same time apply what we have already learned of the
poet and his preoccupations. His frustrated search for a temporary
refuge from the noise of civilization, poignant enough on its own
terms, assumes an additional dimension as we recall the speaker as
one who, in "Home Town," has been driven by equally insistent
urges to seek the shrill and sordid cacophony of a tacky carnival.
Similarly, the poet's meeting with the cardinal, which accomplishes
his change of heart, prepares us for later poems in which he accepts
himself more fully and speaks more assertively. Even more to the
point, the poems in the title sequence, "Heart's Needle," constantly
refer to one another and in some ways require one another for the
full accomplishment of their respective ends. Indeed, Snodgrass
considers the sequence "one poem." When the speaker concludes,
"And you are still my daughter," he urges our admiration for a
resolve and persistent strength that have been tested, season by
season, for the three years described by the sequence. We give it.

Or, to cite a similar example from Lowell's *Life Studies*, only the
uncomfortably intimate knowledge we have gained of the suffering,
struggling poet enables us to sense the positive implications in a

skunk's determined bid for a taste of sour cream. Every poem in *Life Studies* is part of the preparation for an informed contemplation of the whole.

Of course, by the standards of New Criticism, which require full respect for the autonomy of every poem, such perceptions as these might stand indicted for the "biographical fallacy." But the principal working assumption of this critical approach, that each poem must be segregated for analysis, is directly challenged by confessional poetry. It may be overstating the case to call either *Heart's Needle* or *Life Studies* one long poem, the central character of which is the poet, but to do so would be more accurate than to consider them collections of discrete independent poems.

If these two volumes, and others that bear their influence, were but collections of loosely related poems, a second reading would not produce results appreciably different from a first. But the actual case is much the same as with, say, Jane Austen's *Emma*. The first reading, with its uncertainties, occasional misunderstandings, and surprises, is a rewarding, unrecoverable experience, but the second reading, wiser, more comprehending, judgmental, and sensitive to irony, offers different, richer rewards.

Moreover, as we shall see, the sustained focus upon the speaker and poet in confessional poems provides particular stylistic opportunities as well. Just as the reader of *Heart's Needle* or *Life Studies* develops faith in the candor and sincerity of the revelations made to him, so, too, does he develop confidence in the artistic integrity by which these revelations are disciplined and made art. Reading poem after poem, we learn that Snodgrass will not ask our indulgence, that Lowell will not slip into sentimentality, that neither will become mired in bathos. Hence, we grow able to accomodate, indeed, to appreciate the homely expression, the occasional flippancy, or the consciously pretentious phrase, for our context is greater than that of the single poem.

Perhaps the surest indication of the singular importance of the consistent biographical focus of confessional poetry lies in the fact that some intent readers choose to gather together the details of the poet's experience for comprehensive consideration beyond the limits of the single volume of poetry. One critic speaks of Snodgrass "preserv[ing]" in *After Experience* the "self" he has recovered in *Heart's Needle*.[6] Another finds the Snodgrass of *Heart's Needle* struggling out of the swamp of self-pity, only to face in *After Experience* the further effort of ordering "his sense of confusion, frustration, and helplessness within some philosophical framework."[7]

Neither critic is restricting himself to comment on a work of art. Both are, in fact, taking part in the activity that the work of art dramatizes: like the poet himself, the critic attempts to accumulate the poet's experience, to understand it, and to explain it. Such attempts may become reckless, of course, and their results may be irrelevant or misleading. But poets like Snodgrass and Lowell, who have organized the confessional impulse into coherent presentations of experience and character, provide the remarkable opportunity for collaboration in the attempt, not to identify a protagonist, but to understand a man.

One final characteristic of confessional poetry should warn us against easy analogies to earlier personal poems: it has proved to be an exhaustible (as well as exhausting) mode. M. L. Rosenthal quotes Lowell saying, after *Life Studies*, "Something not to be said again was said. I feel drained. . . ."[8] And Snodgrass has said, "There's no sense in doing what you know you can do."[9]

The two factors that weigh most heavily against the possibility of a career as confessional poet are, as the poets' comments suggest, the rigors of the mode and the finitude of its subject. The poet who would undertake, in Rosenthal's words, the "hot pursuit of the realities of his own nature," places extraordinary artistic and personal demands upon himself, demands that some have not survived.[10]

Unlike the Romantics, with whom the "confessional" poets are sometimes compared, Snodgrass and Lowell have described intensely personal poetry not as a form to be adopted now and then, progressively refined, and further explored, but as an intact and nonrepeatable stage in life and art. It may be useful to recall that confession, whether in terms of traditional Christianity or those of Freudian psychoanalysis, is never an end but always the means to a higher achievement. Clearly, both Lowell and Snodgrass, in the years since publication of their confessional works, have turned to fresh subjects and new styles with considerable success.

The question of how confessional poetry may be distinguished within the long tradition of first-person poetry on personal subjects leads us to a second question: How may Snodgrass's achievement as a confessional poet be distinguished within the confessional mode? Part of the answer must come from the next two chapters, which provide analysis of *Heart's Needle*. But we can perhaps agree first on several qualities which tend to separate Snodgrass's work from that of other confessional poets.

First, much of Snodgrass's confessional poetry, like much of his more recent work, attempts what Snodgrass calls the poem of "becoming," the coherent, "place-centered," dynamic poem which is far more like a story than an *objet d'art*.[11] Because Snodgrass's poems often dramatize the individual's ability (or inability) to choose, they accordingly have the particular merit of being able to accomodate and portray change, in the poet himself if need be. Partly as a result, (a "story" must be clear to be effective), Snodgrass shows affinities with such poets as Frost, Auden, and Ransom, who, as Jerome Judson says, "seem to want us to know what they are talking about."[12]

Second, as Alan Brownjohn has noted, Snodgrass generally avoids opportunities to generalize from his personal experiences; he withstands the temptation to make public pronouncements.[13] Among those poets we call confessional, Snodgrass concentrates in his early work most exclusively on the examination of his own experience. His reluctance to generalize does not weigh against the universality of his best poetry, however. As we shall discover, Snodgrass's poetry achieves universality not by any explicit claim, but by the perceptiveness and honesty of its chronicle of private experience.

Third, as Paul Carroll has suggested, Snodgrass, unlike some of the other confessional poets, is not typically a poet of the extreme situation.[14] In the first place, his experiences have in themselves not been particularly remarkable, and he has never attempted to convert the ordinary into the extraordinary. In the second place, Snodgrass has characteristically avoided as poetic material those of his experiences that are likely to have been, at least by objective standards, most dramatic. Thus, in "Heart's Needle," a sequence of poems about his loss of his daughter through divorce, Snodgrass treats the moment of initial separation only indirectly, by establishing a sense of felt inevitability in one poem, a sense of regret in another. His candor is balanced throughout his poetry not by reticence, but by gentleness; sincerity and decorum, the poetry of *Heart's Needle* shows, need not be incompatible. If, as M. L. Rosenthal says, "the explosive anger of Lowell is nowhere to be found" in Snodgrass's poetry,[15] we can find instead the poise and understanding that only a determinedly honest bid for self-knowledge can produce.

In summary, while Snodgrass is like the other "confessional" poets in his sustained close concentration upon the details of his own experience, his poetry at its best is distinctive for the lucidity of its descriptions, the modesty of its claims to public statement, and the respect it embodies for the depths of ostensibly "ordinary" experiences.

II   The Experience Behind the Poetry

The relationship between a poet's life and his art is always complex, but it is particularly problematical when the poet chooses the details of his life as a subject for his art. On the one hand, we can argue that only those experiences that the poet develops in his poems deserve our attention and that they are important only to the extent that he develops them in effective poems. "Confessional poems that succeed do so by doing more than confessing," X. J. Kennedy reminds us. "They arrange language (as well as experience) into works of art."[16] On the other hand, when we are examining confessional poems *as* works of art, we can usually profit from some knowledge of the experiences that lie behind them. Snodgrass himself would seem to agree. "There are a good many poems that I couldn't even begin to understand, if I didn't know something about their authors," he once told an interviewer.[17]

There is a balance to be sought, then, between willful neglect of useful biographical information and fascination with irrelevant details of a private life. We may agree, for instance, that Snodgrass is a "seemingly miraculous embodiment as an individual of the age's stereotype," that "contemporary experience seems to become a part of him,"[18] and that some part of his appeal may well rest in the broad familiarity of the experiences that his poetry describes.[19] We may appreciate the extent to which Snodgrass has steered clear of environments, both social and physical, that would have isolated him from those contemporary ideals and dilemmas that he has shared and described. And, finally, we can infer that many of the virtues prominent in Snodgrass's work—sincerity and careful workmanship, for instance—may be prominent in the character of the poet himself. But in making such connections between life and art as we read Snodgrass's poems, we should be guided by the poems themselves, not by our curiosity about the poet. Otherwise we become literary biographers, and that is an entirely different pursuit.

Still, just as we have reviewed the most prominent characteristics of Snodgrass's art, we should become aware as well of the most crucial episodes in his life, for we can anticipate the major autobiographical emphases of Snodgrass's poetry by recognizing the most formative periods in his growth.

The first is that of his service in the navy during World War II. The war did provide Snodgrass with a few subjects and images that later would prove useful, but, far more important, it removed him from the familiar ties and routines of his home town in western Pennsylvania, it imposed upon him a critical distance from his parents' home, and it made impossible for him the recovery of those comfortable limitations that small towns can impose. "Ten Days Leave" and "Returned to Frisco, 1946," early poems in *Heart's Needle*, suggest that while Snodgrass did return to his home town and the college there after the war, and while he did confirm in a marriage the "ties" that had survived the war, he was a much changed man, not long for Beaver Falls.

We can find in "Home Town" a further indication of the separation Snodgrass sought to achieve from the still powerful lures of his youth, just as S. S. Gardons' *Remains* testifies to a poet's understanding of the destructive forces that can arise in a small town family. But the war itself first broke the hold of the home and imposed an objective distance that the poet could not ignore. The young soldier in "Ten Days Leave" fails to find the familiar security and comfort he had expected. He "wonders when / He'll grow into his sleep so sound again." He never does.

The most significant consequence of Snodgrass's inability to take up again the pleasures of small town and small school was his transfer to the University of Iowa in order to join its writers' workshop. He would receive his undergraduate and two graduate degrees from the university, but more important, he found in the workshop demanding teachers and highly talented colleagues. Iowa was quickly becoming what Kenyon College and Louisiana State University had been before World War II, a center for practitioners of the New Criticism and a place where many of the best young poetic talents might learn from established poets and from one another.

Snodgrass eventually reacted against the preference of the New Criticism for highly intellectual, "academic" poetry. He found that he had to defy (and occasionally dismay) his Iowa teachers to find his own poetic voice. Verbal ingenuity, sustained objectivity, complex strategies of irony—only after training his youthful talent by reaching toward these ends did Snodgrass discover that his first strong voice should be straightforward, not consciously witty, sincere and self-concerned, not ironic. "I'm sure I wouldn't have written at all if I hadn't gone there," Snodgrass once told an interviewer. "I've never been so surrounded by talented, helpful and brilliant people."[20]

Snodgrass's experience at Iowa, a rich mixture of achievement and frustration, of artistic and personal courage and distress, is for the most part the stuff of which *Heart's Needle* is made. "When Snodgrass evokes the dark straggling parks, the tinny Quonset huts, the stinking marshes, spring roads or drifting midnight snow, the July 4th tornado of 1953, the humming hospital corridors, and the God-awful neglected specimens in the school museum, he not only conjures up the buried life we loved," one of Snodgrass's classmates in the workshop says, "but he also blesses it with a rare elegance and authority."[21] Iowa was where Snodgrass became a poet.

But it was also while he was a student at Iowa that Snodgrass had to face the collapse of his first marriage and the loss of his young daughter in the ensuing divorce. This period, in which the young poet had to go about the task of learning to know and live with himself, formed the basis of the two and a half years' chronicle that is "Heart's Needle," a long poem written at Iowa within the developing experience that it describes. As we shall see, Snodgrass's loss of his daughter in this divorce, more than any other episode in his life, forced him to strike highly critical balances—between candor and formal discipline in his art, between self-assertion and loving compassion in his life. These balances distinguish the poetry of "Heart's Needle" and are in large measure responsible for its power.

The experience we should pay most attention to, however, is one not prompted in any clear sense by external events or environments. Even more than his experience of alienation from his parental home, of artistic challenge at Iowa, or of the trauma of divorce, Snodgrass's experience with psychotherapy, first at Iowa, then in Detroit, seems to have influenced many of the most important assumptions, subjects, and strategies of his poetry. He first sought assistance in the throes of a particular dilemma, a two year dry spell as a writer, but he discovered through the experiment in which he participated an opportunity for more than a specific remedy. His therapist, a young resident physician in psychiatry named R. M.

Powell, sought to encourage his patient to express his problems in his own language. But the doctor chose to remain at all times out of sight. Alone in the clinic room, speaking before a therapist who was present but never visible, Snodgrass found that he had to reject, one by one, the pat, jargon-laden expressions he had used to camouflage and avoid his problems. By searching for words he could honestly claim as his own, he was able to define more clearly not only his immediate difficulties, but his sense of his own reality as well.[22] In the poem " $μητις$," dedicated to Dr. Powell, Snodgrass speaks as Odysseus, who has taken on anonymity (as "no man") in order to survive, but who now, with the help of his "dead blind guide," can "kneel by my old face and know my name."

The experience of psychotherapy is a clear source of Snodgrass's single most powerful and influential aesthetic statement, in which he establishes sound self-knowledge as the essential condition of sound artistic achievement and thereby derives "a very old-fashioned measure of a poem's worth—the depth of its sincerity."[23] Yet we should also recognize the importance of the poet's aptitude for the psychoanalytic method that proved so effective in his case. By Snodgrass's own account, the method provided, more than anything else, an opportunity for an arduous expedition into the realities of the self. The initiative, the energy, and the persistence have been those of the patient; the dividends have fallen to the poet and to his readers.

Some years later, while teaching at Wayne State University in Detroit, Snodgrass had to cope with both his sudden fame as a Pulitzer Prize poet and the deterioration of his second marriage. His experience of "deep analysis" there proved, as in Iowa, far more than merely remedial. For example, Snodgrass was able to use one part of his experience directly, in "Matisse: 'The Red Studio.' " In the process of free association that led the poet to his dramatic rendering of the painting's energy, he thought first (as he explains in his essay, "Poems About Paintings") of the rug in his psychiatrist's office; its apparent changes in color reflected, he realized, the projection of his own psychic energies.[24]

But this analysis in Detroit, whatever its specific poetic dividends, can suggest even further Snodgrass's deepening interest in the subconscious as the source of action and art. An informal expression of the working assumption that developed appears in his comments to an interviewer: "Mostly your ideas are excuses for what you're gonna do anyway. They don't really control anything, it's your feelings that control you, that really run your life."[25] This is precisely the consistent premise of much of Snodgrass's critical writing, one that he expresses more formally in the Preface to *In Radical Pursuit*: "Every important act in our lives is both propelled and guided by the darker, less visible areas of emotion and personality. Those, I think, are the resources I am seeking. . . ."[26]

Four experiences, then, in a poet's life: obviously, none of them, including the workshop at the University of Iowa, could have produced a poet where none existed. All have shaped the life of the poet, however, and all are reflected, in one sense or another, in his work.

CHAPTER 2

Early Poems:
Gentleness Speaking Out

THE first two poems in *Heart's Needle*, "Ten Days Leave" and "Returned to Frisco, 1946," are mature descriptions of youthful experience. Retrospective poems of a poet-veteran who shared the brief home leaves and victorious homecomings of a generation, they are distinguished primarily by the quality of intelligence they reveal: Snodgrass joins the veteran's memory and hard-won wisdom to the poet's narrative skill and eye for analogies. Both poems are effective studies of familiar experience. "Yes, it was just like that," we may say, "or it must have been."

In "April Inventory," the last of the early poems as they appear in *Heart's Needle*, the descriptions are of experiences and feelings far closer to the poet's present concerns. Instead of testing his matured judgment in analytical reconstruction, he assumes a strong individual presence and speaks in a direct and personal voice. "*Is* it like that?" we ask instead. The Snodgrass of "April Inventory" is no less gifted with practical wisdom, sharp memory, wit, and artistic skill, but he exercises them finally on the essential subject of his volume: Snodgrass.

This preliminary comparison can tell us at least three things about the early poems in *Heart's Needle*.

First, they are diverse in subject matter, point of view, and style. The short collection includes love songs, reflections on nature, mythic meditations, hospital memories, assertions of identity, and admissions of defeat. The distance separating the poet from the dramatized speaker in the poem varies from one poem to the next. And there is a rich mixture of styles: complex stanza forms and rhyme schemes are part of a structural diversity as striking as the thematic one.

Second, for all their diversity, the early poems do produce an im-

27

pression of uniform achievement. Plain and candid diction, careful
craftsmanship, honest reporting on unpromising subjects, modesty
of judgment, and a prevailing insistence on the truth of oneself,
compassion for others—these subtle virtues combine to endow the
poet's voice with increasing authority and individuality. Snodgrass
earns our trust.

Finally, for all their unity in diversity, Snodgrass's early poems do
intimate a process of development. Whether their arrangement is
deliberate or essentially chronological, the early poems reveal a
progressively greater involvement of the speaker with the concerns
of the particular poems. Moreover, by contributing to our understanding of a comprehensive persona, by adding to our developing impression of the speaker, each poem increases our confidence
in his honesty and reliability, thereby preparing and enabling us to
accept more and more intimate statements about highly personal
concerns.

The early poems in *Heart's Needle* are, then, no random collection of apprentice efforts. They are poems of both remarkable diversity and considerable affinity. Each poem is coherent and independent; together, the poems achieve a cumulative effect. With
Snodgrass, we move from the analytical objectivity of "Ten Days
Leave" to the candid subjectivity of "April Inventory." Only then
are we prepared for the experience of the title sequence, "Heart's
Needle."

I   *"Rich in the loss of all I sing"*

The first five poems of *Heart's Needle* all signify in one sense or
another the loss of secure illusions. The soft cushion of family
routine, the official gaiety of a massive military welcome, the refuge
of psychological anonymity, the sense of all-sufficiency shared by
lovers, the assumption of commitment by those who have been
lovers—such are the usual consolations for man in society that the
speaker in *Heart's Needle* learns to surrender. In his "loss," he must
shoulder a sense of alienation as he exercises an increasingly knowing eye upon himself and his society. But such alienation is not
necessarily a bad thing. Indeed, it is the essential condition for the
life of self-awareness and self-determination, the only kind of life in
which real joy, love, and commitment are possible.

In "Ten Days Leave," a poem that doubtlessly reflects
Snodgrass's own experience, a young soldier (this is the only poem

in the collection in third person, past tense) confronts the mixture of familiarity and strangeness that greets all those who return home changed men. His pleasure is undeniable, so vivid that, as he awakes, he fears he may be dreaming.

> Noon burns against his eyelids, but he lies
> Hunched in his blankets; he is half awake
> But still lacks nerve to open up his eyes;
> Supposing it were just his old mistake?

What he finds when he opens his eyes, though, is his home and family just as he had left them, just as he had remembered them. He knows the names of his old friends, anticipates his father's jokes, and finds that everything "seems just like it seemed."

The only problem is that nothing seems quite real. The trees seem "like miracles," his parents, "like toy trains on a track," the rooms in his house, like restorations intended for the eyes of tourists. His experience of his home is like that of *déjà vu*, as though the familiarity he feels in looking about himself is itself illusory. Or, perhaps, his experience is like "some old film, lit / By lives you want to touch"; the appearance of reality is so vivid that he would seize it, were it not fleeting and inaccessible. Or, perhaps, his experience is like discovering the physical representation of a dream landscape, preserved in accurate scale, or like visiting "a small homestead" preserved to honor the memory of a great man who had lived there. That this apparent search for a fully satisfactory analogy seems inconclusive provides an indication of how intangible and complex the young soldier's feelings are. All that is certain is that, while nothing has changed, everything is changed.

Everything is changed, of course, because the youth has himself been changed by the experiences which have kept him from his home. He returns on leave, endowed for the first time in his life with a critical distance from all that should be familiar. And he finds that, however pleasing and comforting his home and family are, he remains detached from them. No longer a fixture in his home, he can observe it and thus perceive that its offer of security, its show of permanence, are no longer for him. Home and family seem dreamlike and insubstantial in their assertion of order and permanence because these qualities, which once represented reality for the youth, now stand exposed by his man's experience.

The poem introduces the question of alienation, important

throughout *Heart's Needle,* but here the alienation of the young
man home on leave is not from a world now real to him, but from
the secure, untroubled nest he has longed for and to which he cannot return. The recognition which the young subject of "Ten Days
Leave" makes is that he has, in fact, already "left." He cannot take
up again the "sleep" of his youth, in which the perimeters of the
home protect his impression of security and permanence. "He
wonders when / He'll grow into his sleep so sound again," but his
answer is obvious: only when he joins "his folks" as they circle the
familiar track "like toy trains." And that he will not, cannot do.

He can temporarily conform to, or even enjoy, the comfortable
routine of life at home. Nevertheless, just as the appearance of formal order in the poem (seven clearly equivalent quatrains, rhyming
abab, cdcd, and so forth, completed by a couplet) is subverted by
frequent enjambment and radical disruptions of regular meter, so
does the soldier's appearance of easy accomodation with his home
("He will play games / With boys or sit up all night touching
chairs") conceal his restlessness and sense of detachment. In returning to his home, he has learned that he will never be "at home"
again.

It is the usefulness of such knowledge at war's end that is called
into question by the experience of homecoming recalled in
"Returned to Frisco, 1946." The soldiers massed on the deck of
their ship, straining for their first glimpse of the shores of postwar
America, hear broadcast from an airplane overhead the lyric,
". . . you're home once more." Most of them are "home" for the
last time. This will be no ten days' leave. After a well-deserved and
thoroughly predictable fling, they will surrender the drastic con-
tingency of wartime experience for the "old lives . . . old habits
. . . old affections" they had once escaped. For most, demobiliza-
tion will lead inevitably to a renewed concession to the
"authoritative lies" waiting to shape their respective peacetime
destinies. Even their initial "liberty" will allow them only the
dubious freedom "to choose just what they meant we should." Not
surprisingly, the most significant images that strike the returning
veterans are those of a deceptively beautiful Alcatraz ("lavender
with flowers"), and the busy bridge, a closed Golden Gate.

The soldiers are not insensitive to the portents that greet them.
Nor are they naive. Their sudden surge of fear upon hearing the
broadcast greeting surprises them, for they are reconciled to having
their lives planned, even eager for the blandishments of "this

land / Intent on luxuries and its old habits." They expect no surprises; after their final assertion of illusory independence, they will
"turn back finally to our old affections, / The ties that lasted and
which must be good." They will return to their familiar, unfamiliar
homes, and, no longer on leave, there they will stay.

Such straightforward summary casts the poem as a revelation of
the massive surrender of free will to society's "authoritative lies."
The poem's animal imagery ("We shouldered like pigs . . . . We
had . . . scrambled like rabbits. . .") prepares us, according to
such a reading, for the collapse of will that must be a condition of
resubmission to the illusory verities of home.

However, such summary ignores the poem's most crucial element, the mature, comprehending voice of the speaker, who once
experienced the fears and concessions he now describes. The unusual first-person plural point of view permits the development of a
highly individualized perspective on collective experience. On the
one hand, the speaker does not distinguish his own experience from
that of his fellow soldiers; he assumes that his fears and presen-
timents, to be justified by succeeding events, were broadly
representative. On the other hand, he assumes the prerogatives of
an individual's perspective in selecting and ordering the events and
images of a tumultuous day, in conveying the impression of acute
"foresight," and in assuming a critical, ironic distance from the
widely shared assumptions he recalls.

Thus, while the poem may in some sense memorialize former
comrades who have surrendered themselves to the expectations of
their society, it in a more vital sense establishes that someone has
preserved his will and has "lived" to understand and tell the story
of this day. That this someone is also responsible for the poem
makes clear the critical distance that the speaker has been able to
gain from the spiritual seductions he now understands so well. If the
speaker in the poem were lost among those destined to eternal
silence and contentment in the home towns of America, there
would be no poem. Unlike the many who have found comfort from
the sharp anxieties of temporary alienation by conforming to com-
munal will, the speaker in "Returned to Frisco, 1946" remains conscious of his alienation in order to protect and sustain his own
recovered identity.

The process of this recovery is the subject of "$\mu\eta\tau\iota\varsigma$ . . . . ov
$\tau\iota\varsigma$." The Greek quotation refers to the shrewd pun by which
Odyssey secures his escape from Polyphemous Cyclops in Book 9 of

the *Odyssey*. In the familiar story, the imprisoned Odysseus says his
name is "No man." After he and his men blind the drunken
Cyclops, the monster calls for aid. But when his kin shout to him in
question ($\mu\eta\tau\iota\varsigma$), he identifies his assailant as no man ($o\upsilon \tau\iota\varsigma$), a reply that by its apparent absurdity sends the other monsters back to
their respective caves. Odysseus survives, but only by temporarily
surrendering his identity. When he recovers the relative safety of
his ship, his need to reassert his identity overcomes his prudence,
and he endangers himself once again by shouting his name back at
the pursuing Cyclops.

Dedicated to R. M. Powell, Snodgrass's psychotherapist at Iowa,
the poem follows ones that detail the alienation and loss of identity
of the soldier returned home from war. It becomes in context, then,
not a redaction of Homeric incident, but a parable for the speaker's
own Odysseuslike experience.

His warrior's return, like Odysseus' escape, is not without its
price. He has escaped the monster, war, but in anonymity, as "no
man." He has been a "rabbit" scrambling up beaches, a "pig"
pushing against the rail. Again like Odysseus, he feels upon his
return no welcome, but continuing danger and alienation. The oc-
tave of this carefully built Italian sonnet describes the escape; the
concluding sestet is concerned with his return.

> Unseen where all seem stone blind, pure disguise
> Has brought me home alone to No Man's land
> To look at nothing I dare recognize.
> My dead blind guide, you lead me here to claim
> Still waters that will never wash my hand,
> To kneel by my old face and know my name.

As in the *Odyssey*, the hero is finally able to accept, assert, and
reveal himself, but only through the assistance of his "dead blind
guide."

Snodgrass's own "guide," as we have seen, was an experimental
program in psychotherapy at the University of Iowa that, by his
own account, "really consisted of just stating and restating the
problem until you finally got it in your own language."[1] J. D.
McClatchy, whose correspondence with Snodgrass has clarified
such details of the process, explains its implications for the poetry:
"Week after week, alone in a strangely familiar room, speaking out
loud to himself, over and over, the guilts and fears and inadequacies, until his language caught their reality, and problems

became self. And from that self he made the songs to celebrate his discovery." McClatchy calls it "the simultaneous discovery of self and voice, and of the sincerity necessary to both."[2]

But, just as important, this process, as it is projected in the poem, continues the speaker's progress toward, as Jerome Mazzaro says, "action and the future."[3] The pertinent theory of analysis is solidly existential and so fits perfectly the series of early poems in which the frank awareness of alienation becomes a means to an end, the life of self-realization and self-determination.

"At the Park Dance," one of the most prosodically intricate of Snodgrass's early poems,[4] represents a brief interlude in the speaker's movement toward this end. His own interests seem not at stake; the experience of the poem is one of observation, not participation. Yet, the speaker's detachment and the quality of his perception, its objectivity and sensitivity, remind us of his earlier experiences of alienation and of his increasing recovery of self-awareness. It is this preparation, we may surmise, that accounts for his combined understanding of and distance from the comforting illusion of all-sufficiency shared by the various couples as night descends on their dance.

The description of the lovers' romantic self-confidence is beautifully suggestive and generous, if occasionally obscure. The "loving strangers" (strangers to the speaker and, he knows, to each other) follow the firefly's lure away from the lighted pavilion into the surrounding "weathered huge trees." There, the staunch limbs provide a ground where the ephemeral lights, the fireflies, and the lovers merge, indistinct and luminous. The deliberate ambiguity of the collective pronoun (i.e., does "they" in line 10 refer to frogs, trees, lights, or strangers?) conveys effectively the obscurity of the seductive shadows. In them lies "love's vanishing point," where the lovers are no longer corrected by the realistic perspectives of the larger world. They join the famous lover of John Donne's "The Sunne Rising" who, feeling that he and his mistress have become all the world, asserts "Nothing else is." The point of view in Snodgrass's poem is not that of the young lovers, though, so the depiction of their illusion is more cool and objective, if no less just. The speaker's point of view is defined by the juxtaposition of two telling images, one of universal, infinite energy, the other of transience and fragility:

> Beyond, jagged stars
> are glinting like jacks hurled

> farther than eyes can gather;
> on the dancefloor, girls
> turn, vague as milkweed floats
> bobbing from childish fingers.

Both the stars and the girls shine and move in a dark world, but in the difference between them lies the lesson the universe must teach its confident lovers, one that the poet has already learned.

In "Orpheus," the last of what might be called the "preassertive" poems of *Heart's Needle*, the significant themes we have observed in the earlier poems—alienation from the world, the reality of limitation, and the necessity for loss as a prerequisite for autonomous choice—are again important. But their expression arises organically within an artful redaction of one of the most poignant of Greek myths. Instead of simply retelling the tale or manipulating it, Snodgrass pursues mythic and current concerns simultaneously to produce a demonstration of the archetype's continuing validity.

While Orpheus's descent into the Underworld takes him past familiar mythic horrors, the terrain of despair itself, with its ashes, rubble, and "Widows hunched in fusty shawls," is timeless and familiar. His singing wins him access to the Underworld and its celebrities, the victims of eternal punishment, but the song that he addresses to hell has notes that echo in the modern ear:

> "Powers of the Underworld, who rule
> All higher powers by graft or debt,
> Within whose mortage all men live. . . ."

His plea that his wife ("Struck by the snake, your underling") be returned to him seems as much a formal argument against cruel and unusual punishment as a hymnic persuasion: "You gave wink in an undue crime / To love—strong even here, they say." The issue is not their having condoned a crime, interestingly, for they are the archetypal grafting politicians and loan sharks, but their having countenanced an untimely and inappropriate crime against a value even they hold precious.

The consequences of his plea are even more suggestive. As in the myth, the rulers of hell grant Orpheus his Eurydice on the condition that he not look back at her once they have begun their ascent to the world. She appears, "vague, uncertain," and he begins the climb, letting her follow him. But again as in the myth, his assurance fades at the height of his confidence, his willful blindness becomes intolerable, and he turns. She vanishes. His fatal error is rendered as clearly archetypal, for it proceeds from the same deadly combination of pride and mistrust that inevitably brings woe to marriage. Yet, error can reveal truths that temporary success would obscure, and such truths must be faced. Orpheus, we know, after losing Eurydice forever, becomes such a paragon of faithfulness to her memory that he angers the romantically minded Thracian women into murdering him. Snodgrass's Orpheus, though never stepping outside of his mythic role, develops a somewhat more resolute and positive understanding of his loss:

> It was the nature of the thing:
> No moon outlives its leaving night,
> No sun its day.

Orpheus's attempt to recover his wife, though the expression of a worthy resolution, was not meant to succeed. He dares hell not so much as necessity. In facing the infernal powers, he has failed to face reality in the lapsed term of a finite human relationship. The death of love, like that of a loved one, is beyond man's power. But in the painful, regular ("night by night") confrontation with this reality, Orpheus can grow "rich" in his loss, profit from his disencumbrance, and find security in his freedom. Finally and honestly bereft, he can choose to live authentically.

II "A proud rejected man": The Dilemma of Choice

Subdivisions among the early poems collected in *Heart's Needle* may seem somewhat arbitrary. Nevertheless, the first five poems of the collection, by establishing the speaker's resolution to seek an authentic existence, clearly do prepare us for subsequent poems that detail, in one sense or another, the results of this resolution. Similarly, though the next ten poems are largely self-sufficient, they echo associations formed in the earlier poems, confirm impressions of the speaker developed there, maintain the distinctive voice they have introduced, and refine further the expressive capacities of the style used in them.

Moreover, because these ten poems are particularly diverse in style, subject, and especially, mood, the affinities they do have with the earlier poems provide an important suggestion of continuity. Our sense of a consistent persona, derived from the first poems of

the volume, enables us to accomodate the admission and assertion,
inertia and courage, pride and guilt we encounter in the subsequent
ones. Once we begin to know the poet, we can follow him even
when his mood or situation changes.

One other obvious point deserves mention again. Our sense of the
speaker's identity, though largely a function of the poems alone, is
often enhanced by what we can learn of Snodgrass himself. Because
the poems do sustain the poet's self-revelation, we can responsibly
apply biographical information to a fuller understanding of them.
In doing so, however, we begin and end with the poem itself,
always assuming that it is capable of supplying all that we require
for basic understanding. Obscurities in Snodgrass's poetry that can
be solved only by recourse to privileged biographical information
are few, and those that do exist usually do not compel extensive
biographical forays.[5] How often, then, should we apply what we can
learn of Snodgrass's life to an understanding of his poetry?
Whenever a particular poem requires or urges us to do so.

"Papageno" is a good example. That the poem refers implicitly to
Snodgrass's divorce from his first wife and courtship of his second
can be easily surmised. Dedicated to "Janice," the poet's second
wife, the poem is in the form of a lyric by Mozart's timorous but
irrepressable wife-seeker, the principal comic figure in *The Magic
Flute*. We can thus agree that the poem is "about the poet's search
for love after the fracture of his first union," that Snodgrass, "in the
dark and anxious time after divorce, 'went to whistle up a wife,'
seeking love and purification."[6] We may even surmise that
Snodgrass found Papageno's frank cowardice in the face of ordeal
an apt image for his own depressed spirits. That is, we can read the
poem as a biographical document, a symptomatic profile of the poet
at a particular time in his life. But why do so?

"Papageno" is most effective in context, but the important context is the collection in which it appears, not the poet's life. The
poem's relationship to "Orpheus," for example, is crucial. Orpheus,
the archetypal musician, has lost his wife; Papageno, also a musician, is seeking one. Orpheus has spoken eloquently in what proves
to be a futile attempt to recover his wife; Papageno, a foolish fibber,
is temporarily deterred from his search by having his mouth
padlocked. Orpheus, we know, loses his wife forever; Papageno, in
the opera, finally gains one.

Yet for all of these contrasts, we recognize in both poems the
same wry, self-effacing voice addressing itself through closely

related verse forms (seven-line iambic quadrameter stanzas as compared to six-line ones) to the same problem, that of dealing with the different stages of loss and its accompanying loneliness. Moreover, though these stages are dramatically sequential (the paradoxical richness of Orpheus's loss is prerequisite to Papageno's potential gain through willing submission), both poems describe similar patterns of reversal: Orpheus, after unsuccessfully attempting to recover his wife, respects his accomplished loss, while Papageno, who begins his search for a wife "Equipped with . . . fifty linking nets of words" and empty cages, finally desires his own entrapment.

> Night's lady, spreading your dark hair,
> Come take this rare bird into hand;
> In that deft cage, he might sing true.

And both reversals involve modulations in song, for both Orpheus and Papageno are poets. Orpheus sings his way into hell, then finds his proper subject in his loss; Papageno, who has trapped birds for their songs, brings "nets of words" to his search for a wife, but his own song, now the rough noise of his "chattering, blue heart," will resolve into true song only when he is himself trapped.

These many correspondences between the two poems suggest the nature of the contribution "Papageno" makes to the continuing development of the speaker's situation. The search for love, we learn, is not inconsistent with the recognition that love can die; if the speaker as "Orpheus" can sing his loss, as "Papageno" he can sing properly only when he at last is "found." These correspondences provide as well an increasing depth to the speaker's character. If we find Orpheus's courage and sober resolution in the speaker, we also find something of Papageno's foibles, his erring humanity. Thus, by reading "Papageno" carefully, in its context, we increase in knowledge about the speaker's situation and in wisdom about his character—all without explicit reference to the poet's biography.

For an effective reading of "The Marsh" in *its* context, however, some external information can be useful. Except for the final two lines, the poem is a series of images of decay, desolation, and entrapment. Irregular rhythm, complicated by the frequent juxtaposition of sibilants and liquid consonants, imposes on the listener's ear a quality of unrest indigenous to the imagery of fecundity and decay. Though the marsh is alive, and even (in its frogs) responsive to its visitor's presence, its activity seems barely to break the "lull" of its "heavy waters." The muskrats go around in circles; the snail leaves his "ooze" in search of food. In "the enclosing weir / of trees, in their dead stalks," the sun itself "bobs and is snarled."

We do not need to know that these images refer to a real marsh, between Iowa City and Cedar Rapids,[7] in order to find in them a suggestion of the speaker's relapse into apathy and inertia. The painful process of detachment described in "Orpheus" and the search for love at the heart of "Papageno" are both at a standstill. By its sorrowful turgidity, the marsh alerts the speaker to his state and forces him to confront it: "Stick in the mud, old heart, / what are you doing here?" Although there is no answer forthcoming, we may assume that recovery may be made possible by the frank recognition of the malaise.

That the marsh is a real one, however, signals an important shift in the relationship between the represented dramatic experience of the poem and the continuing experience of the speaker. From this point on, the distance between the two will become very narrow and subtle indeed, essentially a function of order and selectivity. The speaker will no longer enjoy a distant perspective on youthful recognitions ("Ten Days Leave," "Returned to Frisco, 1946"), nor will he adopt mythic or literary masks ("$\mu\eta\tau\iota s$ . . . . ov $\tau\iota s$," "Orpheus," "Papageno"), nor will he attain the passive objectivity of "At the Park Dance." Instead, he will be finding poems in his much more immediate experience and developing them as far more direct, if no less artful, expressions of this experience. Consequently, as we learn more of the speaker's difficult passage to authenticity, and learn it more readily and directly, we will grow into a more intimate, knowing, and trustful relationship with a poet who reveals that the high discipline of art can be the single most effective means of sustaining candor, sincerity, and credibility.

"September in the Park" is in some ways reminiscent of "At the Park Dance." But it reveals in its differences from the earlier poem the importance of the speaker's arriving at his more immediate experience. Many of its virtues are familiar enough. No less imagistic than "At the Park Dance," "September in the Park" depends on observations that are, if anything, even more concrete than those in the earlier poem, even as they are decidedly more metaphorical. Accurate naturalistic vision supports the poem's generous reliance upon figurative language. Indeed, if the poem were merely a witty autumnal, it would be a handsome companion piece to "At the Park Dance."

No random collection of fall scenes, however, the poem begins with the careful introduction of its dominant image, the caretaker moon. With its "pinched," waning face, the September moon "spies" the turning maples through the smoke of burning leaves. In one of nature's paradoxes, the smoke is itself made radiant by the light filtered through the leaves that still remain. Later, when the leaves are entirely gone, the "drab, blue-chevroned ducks" flown, the lovers far away, and the bear asleep, the moon will continue its vigil.

> This old moon on its rounds
> of the estate and grounds
>   can well make sure
> that no trespasser stirs
> the fireplace or uncovers
>   the burned out bed
> of ashes.

Thus, the traditional motif of permanence in change: just as the moon's changeability prompts the speaker's recognition that passing time will inevitably bring winter, so does its regularity provide a welcome sense of continuity and order.

By personifying the moon, the speaker is able to project upon it the knowledgeable detachment that he himself assumes in reading the signs of approaching winter. With those who are still out for a late walk, he can enjoy the raucous cries of the ducks, still settled on "minnow ponds still flowing;" but, with his eye on the bare limbs of the oak, he knows the ducks "are going." And he knows that the world of the park "is going" to consign its "furnitures" to "snow's dustcovers," that the couples who feed the bear "will not be coming." Like the caretaker moon, he knows that the signs of fall are all signs of eventual, natural, estrangement: the park visitors, the ducks, the lovers, the bear, and the squirrels must finally leave one another in the park, withdraw from "the ties that lasted and which must be good," and go their respective ways. It is "the nature of the thing." It is September.

The fine balance in this poem between sensitivity and objectivity in natural description, reflected in a comparable stylistic balance between verbal resourcefulness and restraint, is reminiscent of "At the Park Dance." The crucial difference is that here these qualities are grounded in a particular, strongly personal sentiment, expressed in the poem's concluding statement:

> And I, dear girl,
> remember I have gathered
> my hand upon your breast.

This poignant expression, mingling affection and regret, transforms the lines that precede it into a sustained natural analogy for the speaker's delicate and perhaps ambivalent awareness of the "autumn" in a once intimate relationship. The effect is not of pathetic fallacy, for the natural phenomena described are not represented as responsive to the speaker's feelings, but one of sympathetic participation. Like the moon, the speaker is involved in that mutability which bears on human lives and relationships as surely as upon trees and ducks and bears. The park follows and displays its seasons; love, too, has its equally irresistable seasons. The recognition of such affinities provides the dramatic occasion for the poem, a *human* nature poem.

Through the speaker's reading of nature, we gain a still clearer picture of his uneven progress toward autonomy and authenticity. As the poem qualifies and softens the recognition of the inevitable breach abstracted in "Orpheus," so, too, does it help to explain the temporary inertia and malaise recorded in "The Marsh." Not for the first time does the speaker find in nature's changes apt corollaries for those in his life. And, as we will see in the "Heart's Needle" sequence, not for the last.

"The Operation" at first seems not clearly related to the poems which precede and follow it. These have as their common concerns the opportunities and viscissitudes of the life directed toward authentic existence. It records, in evocative detail, the speaker's experience of routine surgery. However, as in "At the Park Dance," the poem's primary subject is not so much the experience itself as the quality of awareness directed to this experience.

The point of view is that of the surgical patient convalescing on the night following his operation. He recalls, first, being prepared for the surgery; now that he has arisen from submission to the surgeon's knife, he can see this preparation as sacramental. Washed and shorn, in childlike purity, he felt (he recalls) none of Adam's shame at his nakedness. In the white garments of unfallen man he could become the "blank hero" in a celebration of healing, a Pierrot[8] achieving pathos in white-faced pantomime, "A schoolgirl first offering her sacrament." The indecision in the dramatized speaker's mind between these diverse roles conveys the creative, blurred vision of the sedated mind.

His memory of his approach "to the arena," the function of an even greater level of sedation ("I was drifting, inexorably, on toward sleep"), is no less accurate in detail, but even more selective and surrealistic. His attendants are at once mysterious guides and royal bearers of the hero through a hell-like cacophony. After the diseased throngs, the weeping, the stares, and the screams, the quiet of being elevated takes on a mystical significance: cleansed, dressed in white, borne by masked attendants, elevated to the arena, the surgical patient becomes, in his own memory, a full and sufficient victim to the surgeon's healing craftsmanship.

Finally, the patient recalls his awakening from anesthesia and the day that has passed in the meantime. In the flowers, the women, the friends, and the nurses, he has met the appropriate welcome for his return. "A small mound under linen like the drifted snow," he has won, in his absolute passivity, the attention and ministrations of all who have come near. Even the world beyond the hospital windows, which would seem to offer in its routine activity a contrast to the still hospital room, is ordered (by a flower vase) for the patient.

It may be, as one critic has suggested, that the poem represents the poet's symbolic rebirth, his conclusive escape from the inertia of the swamp and the ambivalence of the autumnal park.[9] Certainly, those details of the patient's experience that assume sacramental importance in his postoperative reflections strongly suggest the archetypal rite of passage: ritual preparation, the journey to the ordeal, the departure from the present world, and eventual rebirth into a world turned upsidedown for the survivor of the passage. Moreover, such passage would obviously be consistent with the progress toward autonomy and authenticity we have been observing. And what follow are poems which begin to suggest that the speaker's view of the world has, in fact, changed fundamentally.

Even without these archetypal echoes, however, the poem would dramatize the growing depth and honesty of the poet's self-awareness. The experience it describes is commonplace; many readers will find its details familiar. What is singular is the poet's insistence on discovering meaning in an experience that, were it not his, would be routine. He rejects the lie that commonplace experiences necessarily level the individuals who share them, and he demonstrates that, by means of sustained unsentimental attention to such experience, its significance can be recovered. Because the recovery of significance in what is apparently routine and the refusal by the individual to become objectified by any process are crucial to the life of authenticity, this poem is a strong statement of progress toward that end. Moreover, it provides a vivid depiction of an ordeal that, however common, requires no less courage of one undergoing it and no less care and candor of one describing it.

"Riddle" and "Home Town" stand on either side of four poems that detail the diversity of love possible in growth toward authenticity. Taken together, the six constitute both a logical induction to the final four of the early poems, assertions of independence and identity, and an apt conclusion to the middle poems, which describe the uneven progress toward these ends.

"Riddle," much given to the kind of extended metaphors once called "conceits," is aptly titled. Once we know that the poem is addressed by the speaker to the woman who will soon be his second wife, expressions that might in another context sound harsh and cynical relax into a wry, assertive wit. "You have the damnedest friends and seem to think / You have some right to think." The answer to the question posed by the riddle is that the speaker, in saying such things, smiles.

But if this smile finally becomes apparent in the tone of the third stanza, it remains obscure in the enigmatic first two. First, we have the paradox of something so small that only a cooperative effort insures its visibility. As this something draws the couple ever closer and compels the "intergrafting" of their eyebeams ("their sight bifocal, looking through / Each other"), it expands, magnified in their common vision, to force them apart.

This unspecified "it," the crux of the riddle, assumes even more formidable dimensions in the second stanza. The analogy to a playing field, by which the two separated lovers become "goals / That can't be reached," gives way to a much more complex model in which the distance between them becomes "a field of force" charged with their energy. Because their souls are "like," the force between them, as though it were between "like" magnetic fields or electrical charges, seems for the moment to keep them apart. And the poles that together form the axis of this "expansive universe . . . embrace" only at the greatest possible distance between them (i.e., "in circumference") or by the complete break of a rival axis, (i.e., "And by divorce").

Intellective, speculative, abstract, the two stanzas seem an ingeniously associative analysis of an interesting problem. The subjects, identified only by third-person pronouns, are in no way individualized; their reality is vivid only in terms of the metaphors that describe them. They are elements in a microscope, two sets of goal posts, the poles of a field of force.

That they are also beseiged lovers, and that the speaker is one of them, becomes evident only in the third stanza. Unable to sustain any longer his stance of cerebral detachment (implicit in the assumed third-person point of view), the speaker at last allows himself the affectionate banter he wants to share.

The balance between thought and feeling, which produces a strong but even resolution, is most vivid in the dramatic shift between the first two stanzas and the third. But it is subtly conveyed throughout by means of the poem's combining rough, enjambed lines, with apparently random caesurae, irregular in length as well as meter, into stanzas that reveal, on close inspection, complex parallel structures. Not only is the intricate rhyme scheme of the first stanza (*abcadcbdbc*) repeated by the other two stanzas (with a slight variation in the second), but each stanza builds to a short phrase that collects and asserts efficiently its dominant concern. Their arms "Opened wide" in surrender, the couple can meet only by their love "And by divorce."

After "Riddle," we may conclude that "The ties that lasted and which must be good" will no longer bind the speaker to a doomed ("It was the nature of the thing") relationship. But in the next four poems, we discover that the love available to the speaker as the result of his emancipation must itself be defined by analysis and association. The essential premise of authentic life is choice based on candid appraisal of self and situation; the four poems more fully reveal the speaker's self and situation, even as they explore the implications of his developing choice.

First, "Winter Bouquet" celebrates the speaker's joy in the presence of his loved one by considering a striking symbol of her absence, a "dark arrangement" of dry, lifeless plants. He has treasured it, for it was from her hands; its parts were "relics" of their time together. But, as the bittersweet, Scotch brooms, straw flowers, grasses, and milkweed were preserved to provide an appearance of beauty against the coming of the spring, so, too, have they preserved the speaker.

> Those war years, many a wife
> wandered the fields after such pods to fill life
> preservers so another man might not be lost.

Only when the woman herself returns, in the spring, can he afford to scatter the bouquet that has kept him afloat through the winter weeks. In doing so, he celebrates her presence with a public display that thrills the neighborhood children and invades "the neighbors' cropped lawns." The "white bursts of quilly weedseed," as they float through the air, invade his sensibilities as well, inspiring in him the recognition of two contrasting similes: their drift is "like an airlift / of satyrs or a conservative, warm snow." The two images together convey the happy balance of eroticism and comfort the speaker has secured, at least temporarily, in his life. And, just as the memories of war detailed in the second stanza can be related to the speaker's recent personal conflicts (Garapan was the site of a military base where Snodgrass served in World War II), the scene of his celebration suggests a personal victory of sorts. In the hard-won peace to follow, the only airlift of consequence will be that of the weed-seed satyrs, and the snow will be warm.

In his first "Song" ("Observe the cautious toadstools. . ."), the speaker turns from private exultation over the immediacy of love to an artful, carefully patterned, sober approval of its substance. The first of the three equivalent octets, which establishes a strong metrical pattern of alternating iambic quadrameter and iambic trimeter lines, invokes the analogy to nature. In the parasitic toadstools, which flourish in the evening dampness but wither in the sun, the speaker finds a measure of his former self: "Pale and proper and rootless."

In the second octet, which sustains the metrical pattern of the first, the speaker turns from the fragile borrowed life of the toadstools to the utter lifelessness of "cold, archaic clay." Like the antiseptic modeling clay safe for children or the primal matter "before He breathed it breath," the clay rimming the speaker's "blocked foundation" is incapable of supporting any life whatsoever. The recognition of its absolute sterility, though, instead of compelling the speaker to another personal reference, provides a point of transition. If the toadstools, in a sense, indict the speaker's former self, the barren clay directs him to an active search for a more appropriate image for his present sense of shared fertility and personal growth. One is close at hand, and it proves richly appropriate: "The earth we dig and carry / for flowers, is strong in death." In contrast with the sterile clay, which has known neither life nor death, and in like contrast with the toadstools, which derive life by absolute dependence, the "rich / soil, friable and humble," sustains life because it can convert death into new energy. On the ruins of old lives, it can support new.

The poem's turn, which begins with the final sentence of the second stanza, is signaled by a subtle shift in the metric pattern: not only is the enjambment in the last sentence of the second stanza and the first clause of the third particularly noticeable, but the established pattern of alternating seven- and six-syllable lines is suspended in the balanced iambic lines concluding the second stanza. And it is reversed by the four pairs of lines that form the final stanza.

The metric shift calls attention to the thematic and tonal one: images of symbiosis and fertility replace ones of parasitism and sterility, plural concerns replace individual ones ("*I* have been . . ." leads to "Woman, *we* are . . . ."), and assertion replaces admission. Even more important, the image of the tree rising from the fertile corporate soil, "where all our murders rot, / where our old deaths crumble," provides the occasion whereby the experience of past suffering and culpability can become a means toward growth. The speaker and his woman together are the soil, the common basis for their union; but in this union there is differentiation in role, as the figure of the tree suggests. That both participate in one metaphor while assuming contrasting functions in another conveys the mystical illogic that is at the same time the basis and the expression of symbiotic growth in domestic love.

The love described in the second "Song," though, seems anything but domestic. That the metrical pattern of this second "Song" ("Sweet beast . . .") so closely parallels that of the first ("Observe the cautious toadstools. . .") makes even more obvious the differences between them. The homely images of the first song, apparently derived from the speaker's front yard, give way to more abstract ones of darkness and unrest. The conclusive, affirmative tone that the first "Song" achieves is replaced by a proud, almost sinister one. And the compact that is the basis of the first poem's resolution is implied in the second only by the invitation that closes it unresolved.

Yet, for all these differences, the second "Song" defines much the same process as that presented in the first. The life of isolation, unfulfilled desires, and rootless, uneasy dependence prompts here not the metaphor of mushrooms, but that of another night creature, the catlike, skulking poet. He, too, has shrunk from the day. His feline behavior ("prowling . . . I curled and slept all day . . . I crept and flinched away. . ."), revealing his pride as well as his sense of rejection, has prevented his "tunes" from reaching hearers and has thus resulted in a life of isolation and unproductivity. At the end, however, he has recognized the same tendencies in the "girl" ("you've done the same"). On the strength of this perceived identity, he is able to take, just in time ("my love was near to spoiled"), the first measure to qualify his isolation and modulate his solitary howl.

The first "Song" turns on an imaginative confrontation with lifeless clay to effect a transition from the speaker's rootless past to his rooted present. The second shifts when the speaker finds his reflection in the "sweet beast," the girl, though the conclusive offer is prompted only by the frank admission of absolute isolation. Still, both poems describe a progress from isolation to union.

Presuming this relationship, or something like it, to represent the poet's intention, we may well ask, before going further, why a poem expressing in strong and forbidding images the early overture in a relationship should be placed behind an assertion of achieved domestic union. No easy answer is likely to appear, but one may lie in Snodgrass's belief "that every important act in our lives is both propelled and governed by the darker, less visible areas of emotion and personality."[10] In the first song, these areas are barely implicit in the speaker's artful choice of front yard metaphors for his rise from alienation to union. But, in the second, having moved compulsively in dark, animalistic isolation, the speaker seeks release from such isolation only when he identifies one who joins him on the deepest emotional levels, who is, in the dark areas of the personality, one of his own. The two poems, then, are not sequential one way or the other; they are corollary lyrics on a human relationship joined on two distinct levels.

The dichotomy in the speaker's personality suggested by reference to these two levels—on the one hand, his pride in his wide, free "reach," well-rooted in the earth of his union; on the other, his concession of the animallike impulses that have defined his despair and compelled this union—lies at the heart of the speaker's self-interrogation in "Seeing You Have. . . ." Both seven-line stanzas balance the speaker's awareness of the nature of his woman (in the first three lines of each) with his bemused and critical wonder at his own contrary nature (in the last four). This woman, "whose loves grow thick as the weeds / That keep songsparrows through the year," is also firmly rooted, even if she is no one's "tree."

> She's like the tall grass, common,
> That sends roots, where it needs,
> Six feet into the prairies.

But, as the presumed beneficiary of his woman's staunch, dependable, more than ample love, the speaker finds himself drawn, seemingly without explanation, to perverse resistance. He envies "boys / Who prowl the streets all night in packs," even though he fully perceives their vanity and insecurity, even though he hears in his own voice the contentious tone of the quarrelsome blue jays. In wondering at his contrary nature he is not being disingenuous, for his best answers lie finally in the dark forces hinted at by the second "Song." Yet some part of his answer lies in the very similes he chooses to characterize his woman's love, ones that convey more than anything else a sense of stultification, oppression, and encumberance. Before the thick domesticity created by his woman, he becomes again the creature of nature, self-centered, predatory, and contentious.

When he is again in his "Home Town," this part of his nature is subjected to even more thorough exposure and examination. To this end, the poem's apparent organization into seven six-line stanzas is far less important than its logical organization into general statement, general example, particular example, and particular statement.

In the poem's first fifteen lines, the speaker feels himself again a boy prowling the streets of his town. He may be fifteen years older, and wise to the illusions of youth, but "the old hunger" still nags at him: "the old lies are the truth." In the arena of adolescent longing, his age and experience offer him little protection. But the arena is one he knows well, one he understands.

The very acuity of his critical perspective qualifies his admission of vulnerability, however. In describing the young girls as

> hard, in harlequin clothes,
> with black shells on their feet
> and challenge in their eyes,

the speaker intimates the kind of critical awareness that has, by his home town adolescent standards, undone him. That he is alert to the "swagger" and "mutter" of the boys suggests that while the "old lies" may still appeal, they are probably out of reach.

The limitations on the speaker implied by the level of his awareness in describing the general example (ll. 16 - 24) are confirmed in the particular example described in the fifth and sixth stanzas. "Against [his] will," in the face of an obvious appeal from one of the town's hard young girls, he turns away. He cannot accept her challenge, posed in the surrogate voice of the carnival pitchman: "I walked ahead and left / her there without one glance." On the basis of this particular experience, the speaker returns to the self-interrogatory tone of "Seeing You Have . . .," in order to develop the poem's particular statement, a series of three not to be resolved questions that together constitute his attempt to conform his adult perspective to his intimations of youthful desire. His only regret is that, in the particular moment, the compulsion to apparent adult behavior may have resulted not from adult perspective, but from adolescent fear, sufficient to stifle adolescent desire. How can the speaker know? He cannot. Hence, the questions.

> Pale soul, consumed by fear
> of the living world you haunt,
> have you learned what habits lead you
> to hunt what you don't want;
> learned who does not need you;
> learned you are no one here?

In two essays on very different subjects, Snodgrass takes up the function of choice in the adult life. In "Tact and the Poet's Force," he reminds us that "we are ourselves, not by force of circumstance, but largely by our own choice. If we do not approve of ourselves, we could have chosen differently; we can still choose differently tomorrow."[11] This recognition is, of course, basic to the authentic life pursued by the speaker. And in his essay on *A Midsummer Night's Dream*, "Moonshine and Sunny Beams," Snodgrass characterizes adulthood (speaking of Demetrius's fortunes in the play) as the surrendering of "self-pity in being deprived of some imagined love" in favor of "what love is convenient and available."[12] (One might add, a love "thick as weeds.") Combined, these ideas constitute the speaker's opportunity as it has been articulated through the diverse poems, revealing, among other things, the dilemma of choice.

"A proud rejected man," the speaker encounters in the ten poems we have just examined diverse stages in the movement toward authentic existence. He endures a rite of passage, tests his self-awareness against the natural lessons of park and front yard, faces the limits of worthy intentions and the depths of emotional compulsions, probes his own contrarities, acknowledges his inertia, and indulges his anger. Seeking to achieve the life of choice and enjoying intermittent success in doing so, he measures himself against natural and mythic analogues, against the expectations of society, even against his own standards of responsibility. The process leads not to any kind of perfection, but to renewed attempts at self-direction and assertion. The early poems describe no easy progress, certainly, no conclusive success. But it is in the context of the experiences and discriminations they detail that the poems which follow can best be understood; the rich, uneven experience described in these early poems in a style growing progressively more simple and straightforward prepares us for the crucial and complex experiences that the final poems of the section detail.

III *Chosen Authentic Vision: "A Value Underneath"*

The four poems that conclude the first part of *Heart's Needle* sustain its essential coherence. The dominant plain style, combining straightforward, often colloquial diction with expert variations on formal stanzaic conventions, remains. It does become, though, somewhat more distinctive and specialized. The now familiar voice, wry, self-critical, sensitive but unsentimental, becomes more personal and direct. As in the earlier poems, the speaker characteristically stands isolated, physically (e.g., in the woods) and spiritually (e.g., from his students or academic colleagues). He remains alienated. As a result, the issues developed in the early poems, particularly those of self-knowledge and self-determination, remain crucial.

Nevertheless, these poems illustrate, signify, and prefigure important changes. The images they use, the incidents they describe, and the concerns they reveal are clearly more immediate to the speaker and more particular to him. They become concretely, specifically biographical. Poet and speaker converge, so closely that we become tempted to follow the poet's example in using his name.

More important, this biographical specificity alerts us to two principles that become important for Snodgrass and that are evident in these poems. One is that poems should provide for the passing of time: "Time *does* pass in the poems we write now—people change and things happen there." The other is that the poet who is involved in representing "becoming" can relax his striving for "conspicuous admirability." "I want my poems not to be so admirable: I want them to have more of my own absurdity, pomposity, monstrousness, silliness."[13] Both of these principles stand behind a common and most important theme of the final four poems—the uses of alienation. Each poem provides a conversion of some kind, each represents a kind of growth. Together, they provide a conclusion to the early poems and a transition to "Heart's Needle."

The most clearly transitional of the four is "A Cardinal," a long poem that dramatizes directly the poet's shift from frustration and inaction to a renewal of personal and artistic will. Indeed, the poem continues a long transition-lyric tradition by depicting the resolution through a "privileged moment" (Walter Pater's phrase) of the poet's personal and artistic crisis. It recalls in several ways the work by Wordsworth that stands at the head of the tradition; Professor McClatchy calls it, in fact, "Snodgrass's version of 'Resolution and Independence.'"[14]

As in the Wordsworth poem, the poet in "A Cardinal" seeks refreshment in the woods, but finds himself increasingly dejected there and increasingly inarticulate. Wordsworth encounters "Dim sadness—and blind thoughts, I knew not, nor could name." Snodgrass's malaise is similar. He feels like one of society's "leftovers," and the world seems still to be "wrapped with wool / far as the ends of distance," its only sounds the ugly ones of "free enterprise" and "the ancient pulse of violence." Both poets experience encounters, Wordsworth with the old leech-gatherer, Snodgrass with a cardinal, and both, as a result, can assert a fresh sense of "resolution" and "independence." Both poems, finally, are based on actual experiences in the poets' lives.

The differences between the two poems are as substantial as these similarities, however, and more revealing. Unlike "Resolution and Independence," which is the matured fruit of the "peculiar grace" that the poet recalls, "A Cardinal" represents in dramatic form the actual process of conversion. Snodgrass's poem takes place in the present tense, and the poet's voice throughout the poem is that of one undergoing (instead of recollecting) the experience being described. "In the early part," as Snodgrass summarizes his poem, "the speaker is blaming on the society his inability to write."[15] He is resentful in his present frustration, and he sounds like it.

But things can happen and people can change within the Snodgrass poem. They do; the poet does. He decides "he's only trying to blame on someone else what is really a problem of his own internal energy."[16] The result is eventually a poet once again active, one whose voice is quiet and authoritative, one who is again part of his world.

> All bugs, now, and the birds
> witness once more their voices
> though I'm still in their weeds
> tracking my specimen words,
> replenishing the verses
> of nobody else's world.

What happens would seem, of course, to be the visit by the bird. The "sleek satanic cardinal" startles the poet from his bitter torpor and provides the "privileged moment" that he requires for renewal. Just as obviously, however, the bird is no surrogate leech-gatherer, actively enacting a simple but profound moral exemplum before the poet's eyes. The real action in this poem takes place not in the woods, but in the poet's mind, as he converts a symbol of avarice and societal corruption ("join with the majority / in praising man-eat-man") into one of natural, essential self-assertion. The cardinal's song then becomes one worth singing:

> "I want my meals and loving;
> I fight nobody's battles;
> don't pardon me for living.
>
> The world's not done to me;
> it is what I do;
> whom I speak shall be;
> I music out my name
> and what I tell is who
> in all the world I am."

Nothing around the poet, in this poem rich in suggestive natural images, compels him to the change in attitude. He suddenly, quite independently, sees the foolishness and injustice in his making the cardinal the object of his resentment ("Good God! This is absurd!") and begins to look and listen as a poet should. The moment of self-awareness, which Snodgrass justly points out as the *peripeteia* of the poem, proves enabling; the poet can now project a revival of will upon the cardinal, using its example to teach himself what he has known but forgotten, the credo of assertion, the policy of style.

Because this moment is for the most part self-generated, largely independent of any compelling external influence, it manifests the
will that the poet rediscovers as it testifies to the autonomy he will
choose to exercise. In short, "A Cardinal" celebrates the surest cor-
roboration of man's capacity for self-determination, his ability to
change his mind.

It is precisely this ability that the students attending "The Campus on the Hill" have surrendered in order to hold fast to the security they value.

> They look out from their hill and say,
> To themselves, "We have nowhere to go but down;
> The great destination is to stay."

"The Campus on the Hill," which reflects Snodgrass's teaching experience at Cornell, maintains the principles of "A Cardinal," but
its method and perspective are different. The force of time and the
possibility of change are no less conspicuous here—the campus
clock tower commands both the poem and its setting—but they are
objects of resistance for those whom the poet knowingly observes,
not truths that the poet (and his readers) must recover. The speaker
is here not so much involved in making a dramatic personal choice
as he is in regarding the dangerous complacency of those who are
avoiding the responsibility for choosing.

Donald Torchiana is doubtless right in finding the poem a con-
demnation of "the dominant America of the 'fifties, that one great
static, monolithic, irresponsible suburb. . . ."[17] The one specific
topical reference, to Algeria, Cyprus, Alabama, and China, places
the poem squarely in the late 1950s, and the clear picture of the
academy, isolated from the world and peopled exclusively by the
earnest, unreflective students from nouveaux riches homes, must
also be of that time and that place. In its own terms, the poem is a
stinging rebuke to the kind of academic enterprise which protects
the sensibilities of its clients instead of exposing them to truth.
Snodgrass's campus is as empty as the house in E. A. Robinson's
poem, "The House on the Hill," which leaves its observers with
"nothing more to say."

But the poem has a larger significance in terms of the sequence of
poems in which it appears. By dramatizing the critical perspective
of the poet who in the previous poem has laid aside his criticism of
society in a reassertion of personal and artistic will, "The Campus

on the Hill" signifies that such criticism need not be symptomatic of a relapse into malaise. The poet who is sensitive to himself must necessarily be alert to those around him, and this poem is an expression of such sensitivity.

The final two poems, in which Snodgrass again turns his attention upon himself, are even more satisfying because they are even more insistently particular. In both, the speaker asserts himself positively, generously, alert to his own limitations but determined to accept them and to make his choices, name his name, and show "who / in all the world I am."

In "These Trees Stand . . . ," Snodgrass makes such intentions part of a larger subject, the paradoxical balance of inadequacy and self-sufficiency that he has found in himself. "Snodgrass is walking through the universe," the poem's freshest line, sustains this balance. In biographical terms, according to Snodgrass, the line both celebrates a return to the "physical world" after a period of abstraction and acknowledges his feeling that he has not done enough in behalf of values he thinks important. The line also provides him with the occasion to sound his wonderful name explicitly and to emphasize in that way the ever-closer identification of poet and speaker. And it perfectly represents the poem's (and the poet's) complex mood, wry but earnest, playful but serious. "I wanted to write something pompous," Snodgrass once told an interviewer, "while at the same time being *aware* of the pomposity and taking pleasure in it being that way."[18]

The most crucial function of this line, however, is that it takes on, stanza by stanza, the accumulating feelings and ideas of the poem. Like a psalmic refrain, the line signifies more each time we encounter it, for we have learned more of its subject in the meantime. It may be a "very silly line" that the poet discovered "running through" his mind,[19] but it meets every demand that the poem places upon it. The first stanza must serve as the single example.

> These trees stand very tall under the heavens.
> While *they* stand, if I walk, all stars traverse
> This steep celestial gulf their branches chart.
> Though lovers stand at sixes and at sevens
> While civilizations come down with the curse,
> Snodgrass is walking through the universe.

The familiar and poignant illusion described in the first three lines establishes the speaker's ironic, self-conscious self-importance. As he walks through his dark wood, the stars seem to move in obedience to his steps, to accompany him through the trees; "Snodgrass," like any observer, defines the celestial sphere (relative to his position) with absolute authority. But human concerns, by contrast, are not so obedient. Though he is sensitive to the malaise that afflicts lovers and the societies they help to constitute, Snodgrass just goes on "sort of walking around."[20]

The point is not that "Snodgrass" so enjoys the astronomical illusion that he neglects the opportunity for exerting some real influence. One would have to be unrealistic indeed to take on lovers' woes for settlement or to undertake the reversal of the decline of civilizations. The point is that Snodgrass, who knows something of himself and is intrepid enough to name his name before the world, can measure his sufficient existence (for which the obedient heavens provide a fine image) against the candid admission of his ultimate ineffectiveness. Judson Jerome's summary is apt: "I keep hearing him ask, Who are we kidding? . . . Damn it, if I wipe my glasses on my shirt and look as clearly as I can, something endures . . . there is more in me than I thought. So long as I don't delude myself."[21]

"April Inventory," Snodgrass's best-known poem, is the detailed and definitive expression of the candid self-appraisal on which "These Trees Stand . . ." necessarily rests. It could serve as an extended personal gloss on one bit of advisory encouragement in the shorter poem: "If you can't coerce / One thing outside yourself, why you're the poet!" But "April Inventory," as we surmised in looking briefly at it earlier, also provides a kind of summation for the early poems, though it is by no means the last word on the feelings and concerns they develop. It asserts the poet's immediate personal engagement with the speaker's situation, as it exploits the reputation for uncompromising honesty that he has established, poem by poem. The poet's authority has developed along with his distinct personality, so that by "April Inventory" we are prepared to share his reflective, thorough self-anatomization.

But Snodgrass's word, "inventory," may be better, for the poem not only records the memories and feelings of the poet's thirtieth year, but also categorizes them implicitly according to the values he has chosen. The inventory reveals a stock of worldly shortcomings, which the poet accepts freely and somewhat defiantly, a smaller store of personal regrets, and a shelf of modest accomplishments, of assets, that weigh heavily against the accumulated liabilities. Having struck the balance in his favor, Snodgrass can issue a positive report: "There is a value underneath / The gold and silver in my teeth."

The worldly inadequacies he records are primarily those defined by the standards of professional academicians, and the poet's attitude to them may well reflect, as Donald Torchiana has suggested, his ordeal of preparation for "the monstrous examination in literary history for the Ph.D. in English at Iowa."[22] But his sentiments are those as well of an active teacher who fares well enough in the classroom but is too inquisitive, too eclectic in his interests and concerns, and too much a part of the world to compete with the "specialists" around him, the "solid scholars."

There may be some truth in Paul Carroll's charge that the poet at some points scoffs at accomplishments he would like to have made his own—Carroll calls this "the Thoreau complex"[23]—but a larger and more important truth is that the poet has discovered a substantial personal imperative in his distance from the closed circle of successful scholars. His failure to live up to his advertised scholarly projections is less crucial than his success at coming to terms with himself and appreciating the life his "failure" has given him.

> While scholars speak authority
> And wear their ulcers on their sleeves,
> My eyes in spectacles shall see
> These trees procure and spend their leaves.

But Snodgrass, a young man, must also come to terms with aging. Both nature and the university provide constant reminders: all varieties of trees and young women blossom in the spring, the poet's teeth and hair gradually fail him, and his memory proves disobedient. These are all early premonitions of the poet's autumn and, thus, sufficient cause for regret. But the greatest regret that annual inventory brings is the sense of squandered opportunity, of having indulged self-destructive impulses in the face of possible victory, possible love: "I have not learned how often I / Can win, can love, but choose to die."

Nevertheless, the inventory is not complete. What remains are the accomplishments of the poet's humanity—his sensitivity to the people around him, to the world in which he lives, and, above all, to his own right to exist. The value he finds beneath the dentist's gold and silver implanted in his teeth provides the substantiation for his simple credal affirmations, which comprehend the poet's active care, his sensitivity to the world, and his timely escape from the "solid scholars."

> Though trees turn bare and girls turn wives,
> We shall afford our costly seasons;
> There is a gentleness survives
> That will outspeak and has its reasons.
> There is a loveliness exists,
> Preserves us, not for specialists.

Such a plain and unpretentious confession, taken out of its context in the poem (and the volume), might seem saccharine; one early reviewer thought the final four lines "unctuous." But the lines are the fruit of a rigorous and unsparing personal examination and revelation, and in this context, the poet's quiet assertion of "gentleness" and "loveliness" seems understated and authoritative.

That "April Inventory" is specifically biographical in its details is especially important, for the force of its conclusion is in large part a function of its implicit authenticity, its grounding in experience honestly recalled and presented. Karl Malkoff may oversimplify Snodgrass's aesthetic in finding the justification of his poems "not in the poem but in the man,"[24] but he is alert to something important. All of Snodgrass's poems are coherent and self-contained works that require no external framework in order to accomplish their ends. But their ends consistently include the further definition of the speaker, the poet, whose authority increases with the record of his experience and supports the judgments that the poems convey.

Hence it is not at all surprising that readers of "April Inventory" have attempted to search out the names and places behind the poem's references, nor is it surprising that they have often been successful. It may not materially affect our understanding of the poem to know that the child taught about the luna moth is Snodgrass's stepdaughter or that the "song of Mahler's" is probably "*Lob des hohen Verstand*" ["In Praise of Reason"], but such information confirms our sense of the poem's fidelity to the experiences, thoughts, and feelings of a distinct and concrete character.[25] It is in these experiences, thoughts, and feelings that we find the active justification for the assertion which follows from them, and it is because the poet has earned our confidence in his voice that we value his discovery.

Snodgrass's singular contribution to contemporary poetry is, Judson Jerome has said, "the truly individual voice—the sudden break-ing of all posture into a heart-rending plaint for honesty."[26] The development of this voice and the consistent pursuit of honest self-understanding and self-expression within the early poems find their fruition in "April Inventory," just as the character it so eloquently inventories and affirms will meet its ultimate test and find its full exposure in the experiences recorded in "Heart's Needle." "Gentleness survives" and "will outspeak," as this poem says, but the strongest challenges to it lie in the second half of the volume.

CHAPTER 3

Trying to Choose: "Heart's Needle"

T HE ten-poem poem that provides the title for Snodgrass's first collection is the heart of the volume: "Heart's Needle" is the epitome of the poet's success in conveying candor through control, the sustained climax of his concern with intimate subjects, and the consummation of his plan to represent simultaneously the achievement of wisdom and self-knowledge. Although the skill and feeling evident in Snodgrass's early poems anticipate his achievement in "Heart's Needle," the diversity of subject and tone in them suggests that the poet may be moving toward his best subject, his most compelling voice. In "Heart's Needle," he finds both. After "Heart's Needle," and a very few other poems on intensely private subjects, Snodgrass declares the end of his career as "confessional" poet: "I found I didn't want to write that kind of very personal poem . . . anymore."[1] "Heart's Needle," then, is a singular achievement, and in many ways a unique one, not only for Snodgrass, but for contemporary American poetry as well.

I "A Break-Through for Modern Poetry"

As a member of a generation of poets who, after going to war, went to graduate school, Snodgrass was given every opportunity to develop his considerable talents within an approved and widely respected poetic tradition. He joined students at Iowa who, as Donald Torchiana recalls, "had long before canonized the metaphysicals and French symbolists and were most solemn about the sanctity of Flaubert, Stendhal, and James." Torchiana, one of Snodgrass's classmates, remembers their "Authorized Version" as William Empson's *Seven Types of Ambiguity*, their "Logos" as the *Kenyon Review*.[2] In other words, New Criticism still prevailed, and the kind of poems it preferred—ironic, allusive, symbol-laden, complex—was the kind young poets wanted to write. Snodgrass's

58

teachers, many of them masters in the poetry of erudition, provided models and the encouragement to follow them. When Snodgrass turned instead toward a simpler, more lyrical style and highly personal subjects, these teachers, he recalls, "all thought I was wrong, and were really concerned for me." "You mustn't do this, you got a brain," he remembers them saying.[3] But Snodgrass, though grateful for the interest implicit in such warnings, opposed his teachers. In what Robert Lowell remembers as "the most sterile of sterile places, a postwar, cold war midwestern university's poetry workshop for graduate student poets," he "flowered."[4]

Just how Snodgrass came to mount his opposition and to develop finally the style and voice characteristic of "Heart's Needle" is a question that requires more than one answer. Snodgrass himself provides particular credit to at least three different sources.

One is song. What may seem in his poetry a rejection of the tradition of Pound and Eliot in favor of the homelier models of such poets as Thomas Hardy and Robert Frost is often more directly a response to folk and art songs, especially those of nineteenth-century Germany. "From these I learned you could do very personal things, very direct, strident statements about your own feelings, about some specific person," Snodgrass says.[5]

Another was the timely intercession of Randall Jarrell. In a letter to Professor McClatchy, Snodgrass recalls that Jarrell stunned him, during a writers' workshop in Colorado, by favoring some of his relatively simple and straightforward paraphrases of Ovid and Rilke over his "imitation Lowell." "I began to suspect that it might really be better to simply say it, straight out, simply and directly."[6]

And there was, finally, the example of a fellow student at Iowa named Robert Shelley, who began working with a simple lyrical style but committed suicide before he was able to develop it. The style became in some sense available, and its further development by others seemed, with respect to Shelley's memory, "not only permissible but even a good thing."[7]

But the important point, however many conditions we can discover for Snodgrass's choice of his style, is that he searched without apparent preconceptions or preconditions until he had a distinctive subject, "what I *really* think," a distinctive voice in which to convey it, and the confidence to maintain both against the warnings of his teachers.[8] He had learned from them "how to pack a poem with meaning."[9] He would pack it with feeling on his own, attentive to "the only reality which a man can ever surely know . . . that self he

cannot help being, though he will only know that self through its in-
teractions with the world around it."[10]

"Heart's Needle" signifies the extent to which he succeeded. The
ten-poem cycle on the poet's loss of his daughter through divorce is
packed with meaning and feeling; for the most part an Iowa City
chronicle, the poem conveys in an unexpectedly direct and disarm-
ingly lyrical voice the realities of intensely personal pain and
growth. The reality that Snodgrass discovered—his own—was obviously new to American poetry. But also new was his insistent rejection of all unnatural "prettiness," his refusal to resort to "the
voice of any borrowed authority," and his conviction that he had to
convey directly the reality he knew without any manipulation of its
meaning.[11]

Eventually, such principles were recognized as the characteristic
standards of several poets writing on personal subjects, but when
"Heart's Needle" appeared, Lowell's *Life Studies*, John Berryman's
The Dream Songs, Anne Sexton's *To Bedlam and Part Way Back*,
and Sylvia Plath's posthumous *Ariel* lay in the future.[12] In 1959, the
"strangeness" and "apparent impropriety" of the subject of
Snodgrass's title poem attracted attention at once, and his candid,
unsparing voice—what one coy headline writer called the "I" of the
poet—forced contemporary readers to recognize that they had
before them, as Robert Lowell was to say, "a break-through for
modern poetry."[13] Only the potential influence of the new poet,
Snodgrass, remained uncertain, and that not for long.

II *The Achievement of the Poem*

"Heart's Needle" no longer can offer the same surprises it provided for its first readers. Partly because of its own considerable influence, poems on highly personal subjects now abound, and assertive candor is a tone familiar to even the casual reader of contemporary poetry. Those who come to Snodgrass after reading, say,
Lowell and Plath, must wonder at the sensation "Heart's Needle"
once aroused. And it is difficult to remember just why a sensitive
critic at the time would have raised a question of propriety and asked "whether or not the poems should ever have been published at
all."[14]

That the poem is no longer a public and critical sensation is by no
means regrettable, however, for we can now see more clearly the
distinctive strengths which make the achievement of "Heart's

Needle" one of continuing value and influence: satisfactions succeed surprise.

Perhaps the most distinctive strength and enduring satisfaction of the poem is neither the sincerity it establishes for its statements nor the artistry with which these statements are made, but the fine balance the poem strikes and maintains between the two. Packed with feeling, "Heart's Needle" is a virtuoso artistic performance in a wide variety of tough poetic forms. And, as is often the case with musical virtuosity, the strictest artistic discipline seems in this poem not inconsistent with the expression of deep feeling, but rather an essential means to that end.

This balance is not one of the poem's surprises, of course. As we have seen, several of the best of Snodgrass's early poems combine, in the words of an early reviewer, "wisdom and art . . . like man and wife."[15] "Winter Bouquet" and the much longer "A Cardinal" both exemplify the disciplining (and strengthening) of personal expression through the adoption of demanding forms. Indeed, the record of the early poems is one of continued experimentation with exacting prosodic requirements, just as it is one of movement in the direction of increasingly personal, increasingly private subjects. But in "Heart's Needle" the signal strengths of Snodgrass's volume are most highly developed and most fruitfully balanced.

Perhaps more important, it is in "Heart's Needle" that this balance most clearly becomes an integral part of the poem's meaning. From one part of the poem to the next, from one form to another, this balance defines the speaker's crucial distance from the events and responses he describes. The artfulness of each constituent poem, the obvious care and skill which have animated its development, insist that it conveys not raw experience itself but the evaluation and understanding of experience. It is the excellence and complexity of each of the ten "Heart's Needle" poems which achieves that "transmuting" of experience from "private specificity" not fully perceived by some early critics. But it is the progress from one complex form to the next different one, while the subjective focus remains constant, that most clearly demonstrates the speaker's growth from the events themselves to their accommodation within both aesthetic and personal ends.

That painful loss can in time provide a hard-won gain is part of what the poem has to say. But the poem also says that, while time and maturity may provide the conditions for the understanding of experience and its expression, they do not result inevitably in a

diminution of feeling. That "Heart's Needle," for all its careful artistry, is a poem "packed with feeling" expresses a balance in the
mature, reflective mind; this balance between developing accommodation and continuing sensitivity also weighs equally against
sentimentality and austerity. In short, the balance in the poem projects that of the speaker and is part of what he has to say.

This speaker is the poem's other singular accomplishment. His
knowing, feeling voice is so convincing and so consistent that we
can read, with poet Donald Hall, "an emotional autobiography" in
his words. He is no disembodied persona, but, as Hall says, "a particular man."[16] The extraordinary reality of the speaker's personality is in part a function of Snodgrass's decision to write here only of
his actual thoughts and feelings, but it is perhaps even more a function of his willingness to suspend for all practical purposes the distinction between poet and speaker. This distinction, as we have
seen, can be useful in analysis of many of the early poems, including "These Trees Stand . . . " where the poet uses his own
name. But it becomes in "Heart's Needle" an artificial and pedantic
distinction, still valid in theory but pointless in application.
Snodgrass the poet cannot *be* the speaker in the poem (no man can
be comprehended fully in a literary characterization), but it is silly
to call the speaker by any other name.

"Perhaps it is time," William Dickey once said, "for the puppet-
masters to put off their apparitions, dissolve the magical box and
show us what they look like."[17] In "Heart's Needle," Snodgrass
does just this. The poem is the sustained climax of the poet's movement toward explicitly personal poetry; with skill and feeling, he
speaks to us in his own voice. The balance of candor and control
and the sustained voice of the poet, "a particular man"—these distinctive strengths provide an important indication of the poem's
achievement.

Another such indication, perhaps no less important, is that
"Heart's Needle" is at the same time one poem and ten. It is a
collection of ten discrete works, most published separately at first,
each coherent and complete in itself. In each poem, tone and
prosodic structure and imagery are specialized in the treatment of a
particular subject. Each poem has distinctive merits and a distinctive meaning. But "Heart's Needle" is a whole greater than the sum
of its parts. It sustains not only a balance that signifies and a voice
that proves persuasive, but comprehensive patterns of tone, imagery, symbol, and theme which unify it and make it whole.

III *One Poem: Patterns of Unity*

Because "Heart's Needle" is essentially autobiographical, its most obvious unifying patterns are essentially chronological. The poem begins as the poet confronts the "cold war" his marriage has become, the child newly born to it, and the rival, illicit love that he has been unable to deny. It follows the process of deepening alienation, premonition, separation, and divorce, a process which takes the poet's daughter from him. And it concludes in a time of restoration following the divorce, as father and daughter have worked out an accommodation to their situation and have survived, both individually and as partners to their relationship.

The dramatic chronology is further ordered by constant, specific reference to the passing of the seasons. The first poem recalls the winter of the child's birth as it describes the "cold war" into which the marriage has fallen. Frigid images of winter battles in Korea and of farms lying beneath the snow convey both the apparent placidity that the snows can bring and the pain and struggle they can mask. The second takes place on a day in "late April," the fourth ("the season will not wait") describes the early fall, the fifth brings "winter again," the sixth, "Easter . . . again," and so on, through another year, until the tenth poem dismisses another "vicious winter" and acknowledges another spring. In fact, so precisely is the poem developed within a particular time frame that Snodgrass once considered providing specific references for each part of the poem. The first would have been labeled "Winter 1952," the second, "Spring 1953," and so on, season by season, until "Spring 1955," the tenth poem.[18] He did not do so, in all likelihood, because the seasonal references, instead of imposing an arbitrary order on the poem, reflect an order of cyclical development indigenous to it. The seasons provide the ideal background for the relationship in the poem because relationships also have seasons.

Moreover, the seasonal frame supports the poem's abundant natural imagery: a weasel moves "tracking" through winter snows, spring piglets "harry their old sow to the railing / to ease her swollen dugs," "fat goldfinches" fly through "blue July," and morning glory vines wither under an early fall frost "like nerves caught in a graph." Such images, by their accuracy of vision and freshness of expression, are gratifying in themselves and suggest Hall's opinion that Snodgrass has "the best pair of eyes since William Carlos Williams."[19]

Yet these images, like the seasonal references, have a more crucial function in helping to sustain the thematic development of the lyrics in which they appear. The gray remains of summer flowers that line the path of poet and daughter in the fourth poem cannot encourage the talk both need; they are as fragile as human relationships, and they remind both of what the little girl has already learned by her father's departure—that time can take away what we want to keep. Too, the flowers picture for the poet the gnarled outline of a present artistic impasse. But at the end of the day (and the poem), the poet recalls a friend's child who cried

> because a cricket, who
> had minstreled every night outside
> her window, died.

Snodgrass is not insensitive to this loss, but the story does offer him a therapeutically unsentimental perspective on the memory which begins the poem, that of his own daughter's tears at his telling her he would have to leave their home. Images from nature, then, images of death, intimate the poet's own sense of loss and guilt as they reflect for him the pain he has caused his daughter. But another image, also one of death, provides a realistic basis for his accommodation with feelings of personal guilt and artistic deprivation. The *balance* of these two images, that of the frost-doomed flowers and that of the child's lament over the dead cricket, is integral to the poem's meaning and supports its structure.

Natural imagery can also provide links between different parts of the "Heart's Needle" cycle. The little girl who in the fifth poem cannot remember her father's having sung "*Fox / Went out on a chilly night*" seems to him "already growing / Strange," curiously like the severed limb of a fox who must leave behind his paw in order to survive. In the eighth poem, the girl adopts the Halloween costume of a "sleek, fat" fox. Snodgrass shifts the ground just enough so that we cannot form superficial equations, but as the image of the fox recurs, so too do its earlier paradoxical associations of comfortable domesticity, on the one hand, and of painful but essential loss, on the other. The child's visits, the subject of the eighth poem, raise both.

Finally, broad patterns of natural imagery provide a subtle means of unification for the poem as a whole. There are several such patterns; images of animals and those of husbandry provide good examples.

The length of the list of those animals that figure in "Heart's Needle" is itself suggestive. There are dogs and moles (2), a rich aviary of birds (6, 7, 10), a weasel (1), actual and make-believe foxes (5, 8), the cricket (4), a menagerie of zoo creatures (8, 10), the stuffed exhibits of two university museums (9), and spring piglets and colts (10). In this poem we are always with or very near the animals, for they provide a sustained metaphoric context for the personal issues that the poem considers. The few animals that are described as living in the state of nature, such as the weasel and the fox, lead fugitive, brutal lives; they pay the price of their freedom. Those that find secure lives within human society become prisoners, "punished and cared for, behind bars . . . ." David Farrelly states the implied analogy in explicit terms: "Man, unfettered, seems an ignoble savage capable of little but brute appetite . . . . On the other hand, if he is subjected to the ordered ways of society by various forms of physical and moral violence and is forced into a purely mechanical harmony with his fellows, he remains with a sense of imprisonment."[20]

In part, then, the poem is about a man's learning that he is like the animals. But it is also about his learning that, finally, he is not. The poem's animal imagery provides a background against which man can, if he will, exercise the crucial human distinction: "We try to choose our life."

Images of husbandry, which appear in more than half of the lyrics in "Heart's Needle," are closely integrated with the seasonal and animal references and, like them, help to unify the poem by embodying its developing ideas. The child whose mind as a baby was a snow-covered field "unmarked by agony" (1) has become, at three, both more capable and more vulnerable. Her child's garden may survive her ministrations, but its growth will parallel that of her father's impatience to "be away," and its blooming will signify her loss (2). The war torn Korean fields (3), like the frostbitten municipal flowerbeds (4), are apt images for the sense of destruction and loss that is the aftermath of the breakup of the poet's family, just as the sealed warehouses and snug barns of a farm in winter (5) provide a setting for taking stock of what has happened. In the final lyric, the introductory image—

> The vicious winter finally yields
>   the green winter wheat;
> the farmer, tired in the tired fields
>   he dare not leave will eat.

—provides a masterful balance of resignation and achievement, weariness and pride, one that is exactly suited to the poet's feelings at yet another visit from his daughter, yet another spring. The separation has settled into a cycle of such visits, one as regular as the seasons and their crops. There remains sadness and tedium and some sense of constraint in the bond between parent and child. And there is, on the other hand, growth and regular "harvest." But above all stands the recognition that the farm, the garden, and the relationship between father and daughter endure.

Seasonal, animal, and agricultural and horticultural images, then, form sustained patterns that both convey meaning and provide structural support for the whole of the poem. Other patterns, of colors or of images of war, for instance, could also be traced, and all such patterns help to integrate the diverse components of a complex work.

The impression of unity and coherence that such patterns support would be superficial, however, if the poem's images did not reflect so faithfully its feelings and ideas. The images are consistent because the poet is; their coherence directs us to a more important continuity, that of the poet's resolve to describe his experience honestly and, as Snodgrass says, "to write about the emotions that I feel."[21]

It is precisely this commitment to honesty of analysis and of expression which provides the single most important basis of the poem's unity and coherence: its subject. For all its concern with the conditions and consequences of divorce, and for all its loving attention to the changing relationship between the poet and his daughter, "Heart's Needle" is above all a poem about self-determination and the search for the self-knowledge that alone can make it possible. From the first poem in the sequence through the tenth, "Heart's Needle" records "that extraordinary and uneasy struggle," in William Dickey's words, "to get at the truth."[22] Organizing experience becomes a means of understanding it; shaping forms and finding images for expressing experience becomes a means of facing it. The eloquence of the poem thus paradoxically provides the surest measure of its honesty, so that the balance of candor and control, again, not only pleases, but signifies as well.

As we shall see more clearly in the poem-by-poem examination that follows, Snodgrass pursues throughout the sequence the same end—a sense of his own identity as a creature not of habit, but of choice. This constant pursuit gives rise to related principles of continuity. Robert Phillips identifies "alienation" and "love" as the poles between which the drama of the poem (and that of the entire volume) moves.[23] "Oppositions," for Richard Howard, provide the substance of the poet's progress through confrontations toward unification of his personality and his art.[24] Neither is wrong, but such principles are subsidiary to a far broader one, the poet's insistence on knowing the only reality he can, "that self he cannot help being," through the examination and description of that self in interaction with the world.[25] His particular experience with the loss of his daughter through divorce provides Snodgrass the opportunity of limiting and intensifying his pursuit, but it is the pursuit itself that remains constantly at the center of the poem. Professor McClatchy makes the point well: "As both a completely other person and still a part of himself, his daughter provides Snodgrass a unique occasion to confront his self at a point where all its relationships converge."[26]

"We try to choose our life," Snodgrass tells his daughter. But choice, authentic choice, depends upon self-knowledge, and self-knowledge depends upon the absolute commitment to honesty. The measure of a poem is the measure of a life, "the depth of its sincerity."[27] The wise and honest and well-crafted poem becomes both a means to and evidence of progress toward the authentic life of conscious choice. As such, "Heart's Needle" is most truly "one poem."

IV *Ten Poems: Realized Responses*

Analysis of "Heart's Needle" as "one poem" necessarily must reveal many of the special strengths of its constituent poems, for it is the particular success of each which sustains that of the whole. Similarly, poem-by-poem analysis, while it concentrates on meaning and expression specific to each distinct work, offers a further opportunity for appreciation of the unity and coherence of the sequence.

(1) The first poem, a long run-on sentence that has been justly described as an "overture" to the whole of "Heart's Needle," begins by introducing the "only daughter . . . the needle of the heart," the poet's child, Cynthia.[28] Her birth, recalled here nearly three years later, may have necessitated an armistice in the "cold war" of her parents' failing marriage, but it has failed, clearly, to produce anything like a real peace. The agony of the poet, who even as he became a father

was torn

> By love I could not still,
> By fear that silenced my cramped mind. . .

continues. In associating his daughter's birth with the bitterest winter of the Korean War, "When the new fallen soldiers froze / In Asia's steep ravines and fouled the snows," the poet does not insist that his suffering has been equivalent to that of the soldiers, but his direct association of the two indicates the extent of his plight.

The poet's only present consolation is that his daughter, her infant's mind "a landscape of new snow," has so far been spared the hurt of the continuing "cold war." Like the "chilled tenant-farmer," watching over his snow-covered, rented fields, he can regard his "land / Unmarked by agony, the lean foot / Of the weasel tracking, the thick trapper's boot." But his child is growing, and the winter provides other reminders as well. The snow may recall to the poet the quilts in the maternity ward, but such quilts are also used to cover beds of pain. Even more ominously, the unmarked snow seems to the poet a blank page awaiting the print of his will. Winter will pass; the poet's daughter will become more and more vulnerable to the choices he must make; the cold war is unbearable.

In the context of this developing crisis, the poem introduces the central concern of the sequence: lost in his cold war, he says, "I could not find / My peace in my will." The allusion to Dante's *Paradiso* implies that the problem at issue is not the simple one of being uncomfortable in following one's wishes; the problem is one of recognizing both the fearful power of the independent will and one's responsibility for the exercise of this power in the making of deliberate, informed choices. In the *Paradiso*, Piccarda tells Dante that peace comes to the blessed because their respective wills are engulfed by and incorporated within the will of God: "the King . . . draws our wills to what He wills; and in His will is our peace." But as no such peace seems available to Snodgrass, Piccarda's earlier words may be even more ironically pertinent to his plight: "Brother, the power of love [of God] quiets our will and makes us wish only for that which we have and gives us no other thirst."[29] For Snodgrass it is the human love he "could not still" that has had precisely the opposite effect: this love has become something he does not have but wants desperately, something he cannot have unless he arouses and exercises *his* will.

Yet the poet understands the implications of seeking peace in his will. His daughter, so far "unmarked" by the cold war of his marriage, will not remain so if he goes his own way. Hence, the poet concludes with an uneasy resolution to make a last attempt to live within the terms of the armistice:

And I have planned

My chances to restrain
The torments of demented summer or
Increase the deepening harvest here before
It snows again.

Restraint on the one hand, renewed involvement on the other—these seem his last chances.

The concerns of the poem are so clear, the images so vivid, and the syntax so unpretentious that its remarkable skill in accommodating a single, complex statement to the rigid structure of regular, rhymed quatrains (*abba, cddc,* and so forth) is unobtrusive throughout. But not unimportant. As we should by now expect, a subtle manifestation of control establishes the work's authority; it represents part of that signifying balance which projects the poet's capacity for understanding and expressing his experience. But the effects of this control are even more far-reaching. The rhymed quatrains, far from retarding the development of the poem's statement, accelerate it. End stops and pauses between the quatrains, natural to a stanzaic form, are spanned by the developing meaning of the poem's statement, while many of the caesurae that the syntax might provide are minimized in their effect by the prosodic momentum. Sound echoes sense. The poet would hold off the inevitable and stand by winter. The largely subliminal message in the poem's music is that spring will not wait.

(2) In the second poem, spring has arrived and, with it, a clear sense of coming separation. Summer torments must seem unavoidable, further restraint, impossible. The father and poet seems to have already decided to choose. Now he must act. But because he remains both father and poet in this most precarious existence—still at home though now committed to leaving—he must continue for the moment the loving rituals of parenthood, even as he must face their larger meaning in terms of his particular dilemma.

The ritual here is the planting of the child's flower garden. As if he were addressing himself in the present tense to his daughter,

Snodgrass wryly records the day's achievement: the garden has been dug, wholly inadequate defenses have been erected against its enemies, and it has somehow survived the three-year-old's overzealous ministrations. It will bloom.

But because it will bloom after the poet has at last made his departure, the flower garden assumes a twofold symbolic significance for him. First, the gardener's responsibilities recall the parent's; both must find the right balance between underprotection and excessive care if "young sprouts" are to thrive. The poet, who is prepared to relinquish at least part of the father's responsibility in the "cultivation" of his daughter, takes stock of far more than the day's tasks when he concludes, "Child, we've done our best." Someone will have to continue this work, just as someone will have to weed and thin and water the seedlings, but it will not be the poet. Second, the garden's growth must signify the arrival of the summer, which the poet now associates with his inevitable leavetaking. Although the daughter cannot know it, her flowers will measure her father's last days at home:

> You should try to look at them every day
> Because when they come to full flower
> I will be away.

The final sentence of the poem provides its only explicit reference to the theme of self-determination, but Snodgrass again relies on tacit associations aroused by concrete images to convey much of the feeling contained within the poem. "Strange dogs at night and the moles tunneling" are common garden foes, but their furtive destructiveness makes them images of the father's parental anxieties as well. Similarly, the mixed seeds, planted to outlast the father, to flower as he fades, seem to him, by an implied comparison, "steadfast" in their rows.

And the music of the poem again sustains a significant part of its meaning. The regular sestets, as they establish and sustain a fluid iambic tetrameter, help to provide an initial impression of comfortable domesticity. A nice poem about a nice day. But the meter soon becomes less comfortable, as does the feeling in the poem: the caesurae become more and more variable, the fourth line of each stanza grows into a pentameter, and the final line shrinks to a terse trimeter. This art, as it conceals its effects, allows no escape from them.

(3) By the occasion of the third poem (to which Snodgrass once gave the title "The Separation"), the poet has left his wife and relinquished his daughter. He has chosen. But instead of offering a settled explanation for a completed action, the poem bears the signs of continuing unrest. The poet seeks through it the specific assurance that his leavetaking has been an expression, not a denial, of parental love and responsibility.

To this end, he examines three sharply different episodes: an observed moment of parental teamwork, the settlement of the Korean War, and a small playtime injury he once inflicted on his daughter. In the immediate aftermath of his losing his daughter, he is able to find bitter associations in benign images and tenuous parallels in horrific ones.

The first stanza is devoted to a straightforward, carefully drawn account of a couple lifting a child over a puddle. It is in one sense artful and charming, the "lurch" of one line emphasizing the swinging iambs of the next. But set against what the poet has already told us about his child and his marriage, the glimpse of the swinging child provides a symbolic model of the child's place in the collapse of the poet's marriage. The "live weight" which at one time pulled man and wife together now requires that they pull apart, though the weight remains and both must still maintain it.

The heart of the poem, more than three of its six stanzas, suggests an elaborate parallel between the final stages of the Korean War and those of the failed marriage. Stalemated, futile hostilities, whether the battlefield be Korea or the poet's home, bring only agonizing frustration: "The whole jaw grinds and clenches / Till something somewhere has to give." Any concessions are preferable to this, even the division of a nation or a family. But the concessions themselves are exacting and painful: "It's best. Still, what must not be seized / Clenches the empty fist."

The exchange of clenched jaw for clenched fist may seem a poor reward for separation, especially in the poet's case, but, as his memory of a minor accident suggests, the interests he has attempted to protect have been not solely his own. He knows what tugging on a child can do. In play, he once dislocated his daughter's wrist. But the tugging that can arise in the breaking up of a family is far more dangerous. Rather than risk serious injury to his daughter, the poet has had to surrender her: "I've gone / As men must and let you be drawn / Off to appease another . . . ." The paradox that a man may exercise his responsibility by appearing to abdicate it proves the sure sign of love, one with powerful precedents:

> It may help that a Chinese play
> Or Solomon himself might say
> I am your real mother.

The allusion to Solomon, who awarded an infant to its rightful mother by choosing the woman who would surrender it before seeing it divided for equal distribution, forms a just conclusion to the poem's myriad images of loveless tugging. The poet in this case will not win the child, but he emerges with a crucial victory nevertheless, self-knowledge sufficient to allow him to approve his own choice. He has left the home in which his daughter lives, but he is still her father. Even more so.

(4) We have already examined how the natural images in "Heart's Needle" reflect the sorrow of father and daughter as they settle awkwardly into the routine of approved visits. We have noticed as well how the father's sense of inadequacy and guilt has additional consequences in the poet's frustration: the scrawling morning glory vines, half dead by frost, seem "Like broken lines / of verses I can't make." And we have observed how the final stanza "gently displaces" (in Professor McClatchy's phrase) the melancholy and anxiety of the first six with a poignant anecdote, one that provides a healing recognition for both gloomy father and struggling "minstrel."

We might, then, look more closely in this poem at the ways in which sound makes sense, or at least at the ways we can begin to understand. (Much of a poem's music, as Snodgrass has said, "is something so deep that almost no one ever knows what it means."[30])

The stanzaic form Snodgrass chooses is unusually demanding: the stanza breaks down aurally into a quick succession of trimeters (*aba*) followed by a rhyming pair of lines (*bb*) in which a leisurely tetrameter is matched with a compact, often striking, bimeter.

The third stanza illustrates one way in which such a complex, well-realized form can support the effects of more limited prosodic devices:

> We huff like windy giants
> scattering with our breath

> gray-headed dandelions;
> Spring is the cold wind's aftermath.
> The poet saith.

The first three lines, all with three strong though not perfectly regular beats, describe the actions of poet and daughter by simulating them. "Huff . . . breath . . . gray-headed"—such aspirates can themselves scatter dandelion seeds. And the accentual irregularities, such as the final syllable in the first line or the dactyl that begins the second, support the sense of "puffing" against that of regular rhythmical breathing. Both effects are delightfully consistent with the playful bombast of the simile, in which the adjective ("windy") deflates the "giants."

The shift to a tetrameter in the fourth line brings a shift in tone as well, from the informal account of personal experience to the formal diction of a somewhat "windy" aphorism. The semicolon signifies a real logical coherence—the dandelion seeds father and daughter scatter to fly in the cold wind will spread to arise as early signs of spring—but only makes the tonal discrepancy the more obvious. This discrepancy is, of course, part of the stanza's calculated effect. Applied to present circumstances, the timely poetic saw seems sadly incongruous, even (as the short, conclusive attribution in the bimeter suggests) a bit archaic. In his present situation, breathless in a happy moment within a strained occasion, the poet finds useful old sayings useless. He must look further to find the anecdote that meets his needs precisely.

(5) Halfway through the "Heart's Needle" sequence, the poet returns to winter, to his daughter—even, it would appear, to his former home. But the poem is about acknowledging the distance that return can reveal, not about overcoming it. Snodgrass once considered titling the poem "Loss of Feeling."

At first, the subject of the poem seems to be the poet's awareness of changes in his daughter:

> You chatter about new playmates, sing
> Strange songs; you do not know
> *Hey ding-a-ding-a-ding* . . .

She does not remember the old bedtime rituals, and she no longer seems concerned about the "squalls and storms" that still arise between her parents. After only a half year's separation, the poet

finds his daughter "already growing / Strange." Robert Phillips has
suggested that this strangeness is reflected even in the prosody, as
the "halting enjambment" in the run-on lines conveys "emotionally
not only the girl's physical development but also her increasing
mental alienation from her father."[31]

The primary subject of the poem, however, is the father and poet
himself. As the central metaphor of the fox suggests, the poet's
recognition of the developing estrangement is most at issue. The
poet associates himself with the fox subtly at first, by recalling the
song he would sing his daughter ("Fox / Went out on a chilly
night") before going out himself on chilly nights. Both fox and
father know what it is like to leave the lair "in a hungry plight" for
night wanderings: "I have gone prowling" sings the "stray" in
"Song").

But the association becomes critical only as the poet turns from
reminiscences of the fox in the song to a frightful imaginative mental picture of the one in the fields. As the snow, of time as of winter,
obliterates the signs of the father's imprint, it swirls as well

> Beyond to the blank field,
> The fox's hill
>
> Where he backtracks and sees the paw,
> Gnawed off, he cannot feel;
> Conceded to the jaw
> Of toothed, blue steel.

Like the fox, the poet has doubled back to observe once again the
loss he has sustained in order to be free. He has escaped the trap of
a failed marriage, but only by leaving a part of himself behind. The
crucial word is "conceded," which is so dispassionate that, as it
states the event of the loss, it suggests as well the poet's (and the
fox's) growing distance from it. Such a sacrifice, for poet or fox, can
become a "concession" only when "loss of feeling" becomes a feeling itself.

(6) One measure of the faithfulness of "Heart's Needle" to
human reality as the poet has experienced it is that it depicts no
smooth course in the poet's achievement of either self-knowledge or
self-determination. The poet acts after expressing the hope of put-
ting off the necessity to act. Having acted, he seeks justifying images and precedents and settles upon small consolations. Then, as
time provides some sense of distance, he notices "loss of feeling."

With the end of the first half of the sequence, the poet's struggle, at least with regard to "the needle of the heart," seems very nearly complete. But spring (and the sixth poem) brings renewal—of nature, of memory, of feeling, of resolve, and of confrontation.

Snodgrass began this poem, he says, by gathering "a set of reminiscences and images about Easter, rebirth and repetition, eggs, birds, and flight."[32] Working with a complicated stanzaic form he had admired in works by other poets, he organized these images into a vivid and suggestive montage. The first version of the poem, as it introduced most of the scenes prominent in the final form, revealed much about the poet's state of mind. Snodgrass explains:

The image of hacking the limbs off the trees was related to my separation from my daugher . . . ; the pigeon fluttering out of my hands was related both to my letting her go in the separation and also to the way she sometimes ran away to make me chase her. The blackbird in the last stanza [the fourth in the finished poem] seemed to be my first wife "protecting" her nest; the killdeers crying over their flooded nests implied some sense of grief over the breaking up of the home.[33]

But Snodgrass was not satisfied. He could find no clear pattern in the poem, and he was not sure why he had wanted to use Fourth of July memories in an Easter poem.

Later, Snodgrass began to feel that his first version had only barely intimated the concern that was in fact dominating his feelings; conversely, the grief prominent in the poem was not equally prominent in the poet's thoughts.

One Fourth of July had brought a storm to Iowa City, and it had threatened Snodgrass's daughter; but more important for this poem, the same holiday one year later had brought the death of Snodgrass's asthmatic sister, a strangely inexplicable death much like that which is the subject of S. S. Gardons' *Remains*. "Neither her asthma nor any of its complications appeared severe enough to end her life—not if she had really wanted to go on," Snodgrass says.[34]

While working on the poem, Snodgrass was particularly distressed by his sister's death, for he saw in it the perverse exercise of her will—"man alone has the choice to withdraw from the reality in which he lives, and so has the power to die"—and he feared the same will might be developing in his young daughter from her continuing anger over the loss of her father. He feared that an asthma attack she had suffered "was *her* way of refusing her life." Thus, Snodgrass concluded, "I felt that I must find some way to tell her that she must choose what reality was possible—that she was, of course, full of rage and regret for what she could not have, but that she was hardly alone in that. She still must choose what was unavoidable. This was the particular rebirth I wanted that year."[35]

By this recognition, Snodgrass understood that his references to the Fourth of July, with the images of tangled, damaged limbs waiting to be freed by the powersaws, sustained his overriding concern with freedom and guilt and called for two further stanzas, one dramatizing his daughter's asthmatic symptoms, the other providing straightforwardly the poet's message to his daughter:

> Of all things, only we
> have power to choose that we should die;
>   nothing else is free
> in this world to refuse it. Yet I,
>   who say this, could not raise
>   myself from bed how many days
> to the thieving world. Child, I have another wife,
> another child. We try to choose our life.

The poem concludes not with the poignant image of the killdeers, as did the first version, but with a surprisingly direct lesson about man and the faculty of choice which he can and must exercise. The statement proves to be what Snodgrass had all along wanted to deliver. In the process of making a better poem, one "more personal and so more universal," Snodgrass found, he says, "what I needed to say."[36]

His discovery is, moreover, one that reflects upon the whole of the sequence, just as the sixth poem signifies an important transition in it. The memories the daughter brings along with her Easter egg and the images her presence inspires force the poet to recognize that the "loss of feeling" which time can provide is an undependable and finally unworthy basis of accommodation to the results of decisive choices. By facing and expressing directly the grounds for his continuing anxiety, the poet is able to articulate clearly for the first time the rationale by which he has decided to live: "We try to choose our life." After this point, the poet, both as creator and as character in the poem, is a man more self-aware and, though still vulnerable to feelings of guilt, more free. The poem is thus both a statement of dramatic movement within the sequence and a record of personal growth. Through revising, Snodgrass says, "You have approached something basic to that pattern of ideas and emotions and feelings which *is* your mind; you find out something of what *your* meaning is."[37]

(7) In the "summer" poem, the poet's hard-won understanding yields a single, just image:

> I lift you on your swing and must
> shove you away,
> see you return again,
> drive you off again, then
>
> stand quiet till you come.

The poem is itself a swing: the left margin oscillates backwards and forwards as the lines carry the poet's daughter slowly to the top of her arc, pause momentarily in a feminine rhyme, and return her quickly then to the poet's hands:

> You, though you climb
> higher, farther from me, longer,
> will fall back to me stronger.

The poet's extraordinary skill and honesty, still effectively balanced, are enhanced here by his developing wisdom. By means of his effort to choose his life and to understand the choices he makes, he has begun to develop an appreciation for his problematical relationship with his daughter. He knows the sense of equilibrium that a regular routine of visits and leavetakings can provide, just as he knows that this routine will probably have to be modified in favor of visits fewer and further apart. He knows the lessons of the snarled limbs and the pigeon net. He will want to hold his daughter and must do so, but he knows now that he also must push her away so that, in a loving oscillation of affection and distance, of control and freedom, she will be able to thrive on her difficult life and become strong.

(8) On the summer playground, the poet enjoys a moment of particular happiness. His hard-won understanding of himself and the choices he has made affords him the gentle authority that the image of the swing represents perfectly. He and his daughter are partners in a common enterprise; its end is their respective growth. But when his daughter returns to him for a visit during Halloween

week, the partnership founders, and the poet finds his sense of
authority and assurance undermined once again. As confrontation
takes the place of camaraderie, the poet's apprehensions for his
daughter assume a familiar form: "Assuredly your father's
crimes / are visited / on you."

The grounds of the confrontation seem trivial. Having eaten too
much trick-or-treat candy, the poet's daughter refuses the meal he
has prepared. "By local law," she must then take her meals in her
own room. Her resistance continues. To the poet, the conflict is fundamental, for it bears on his responsibility and right to "nourish"
his child. Moreover, it provokes the fear that the strengths he has
been able to impart to her are proving destructive. An argument
over a loss of appetite provides the terms for the entire poem, as it
moves the poet to consider the problems he has encountered during
the child's short lifetime in trying to provide what she must have.

First, he recalls difficulties with infant feeding. Sour milk finally
proves effective. But then, in the early months of the father's
separation from his family, the restaurant meals and sack lunches he
provides for her as an older child dramatizes for them both how far
they are from the family table. In her child's fashion, she wants a
romantic dinner, and so asks her father to catch a low-flying star,
"pull off its skin / and cook it for our dinner." But the father cannot
provide. At the zoo, at least, they find pleasure in feeding the
animals, if not each other. Finally, the poet learns to cook a few
things himself, so that, even as he asks his daughter to visit him less
often, he can set a table for her when she does.

Surfeited with Halloween treats, though, the daughter refuses his
food. Her father's child, she has prowled the neighborhood in the
disguise of a fox. And she has preferred the candy provided by
strangers, or so it would seem, to the loving meal awaiting her at
home. Hence, she is separated again from the "family" table: "I set
your place on an orange crate / in your own room for days." At
night, she grates her jaw.

The insurrection drives the poet once more to fears that his
choices may weigh against hers, that his "crimes" will be punished
in her. As David Farrelly has suggested, Snodgrass's general
reference to the Old Testament notion of hereditary responsibility
may contain a more pointed allusion to the well-known proverb that
Ezekiel and Jeremiah cite: "The fathers have eaten sour grapes, and
the children's teeth are set on edge."[38] His daughter, who once
could digest only sour milk, lies asleep, her teeth on edge.

The lesson this unhappy incident teaches is
already taken to heart: "the only possible an
come here less." She is for him the "sweet f
appetite and, like the candy that he craves,
No more promising conclusion is possib
cumstances. Snodgrass once gave the po
"Ferment."

(9) With the return of winter, the poet sinks into an even deeper
malaise. Though the weather is not yet that cold, he feels "numb."
His daughter, for the first time in the sequence, is conspicuously ab-
sent, and he for the first time feigns and perhaps wants to feel a
measure of indifference. But the poem itself, as it is addressed to the
poet's daughter, weighs against this impression. The poet is in fact
obsessed with the "deadlock"[39] he describes at the poem's conclusion:

> Three months now we have been apart
> less than a mile. I cannot fight
> or let you go.

It is this obsession, compounded of continuing practical anxieties,
particular regrets, general remorse, and above all, a pervasive
taedium vitae, for which the poet seeks objective images. He finds
most of them in a museum (actually, two museums, in Iowa City
and Ithaca, New York) of natural history—first among the stuffed
animals of public displays, then among the horrific specimens in an
exhibit of morphological malformations. By gathering these images
and examining the associations they raise, the poet would seem to
make his despair only more substantial. The more he sees and the
more he thinks about what he sees, the more he feels compelled to
admit, "I don't know the answers." His experiences and reflections
arouse him finally to the most bitter vision in "Heart's Needle":
"The world moves like a diseased heart / packed with ice and
snow."

Yet the poem is no simple projection of despondency. That would
be no poem at all, or a very bad one. Because the poem's
protagonist is also its craftsman, the sharp perceptions and just
associations it contains provide one subtle but critical piece of additional information about his plight: at his most wretched, when
the world presents to him only reminders of universal misery, the
dramatized poet, the speaker, remains in firm control of his craft. At

int, for instance, he discovers in a diorama the right images
for the contentiousness of his daughter and stepdaughter and
his own inexplicable insistence on resolving their momentary
spat by a show of parental force:

> Here in the first glass cage
> the little bobcats arch themselves,
> still practicing their snarl
> of constant rage.
>
> The bison, here, immense,
> shoves at his calf, brow to brow,
> and looks it in the eye
> to see what is it thinking now.

At another point, despondent that his efforts for his daughter seem
futile and sterile ("I write you only the bitter poems / that you can't
read"), the poet raises, in eloquent condensation, the archetypal account of mean and wasteful self-service:

> Onan who would not breed
> a child to take his brother's bread
> and be his brother's birth,
> rose up and left his lawful bed,
> went out and spilled his seed
> in the cold earth.

The poet is in every sense a prisoner of dry, bleak midwinter. The
weather, the envious possessiveness of his former wife ("the lean
lioness . . ."), the tensions between his two families, the stuffed
animals, the bottled specimens, and the clouding window all weigh
heavily against his spirit, and this poem "of total awareness"[40]
faithfully describes every such burden. But the poet's artistic
strength, by its exercise in the poem, testifies to yet a further incre-
ment of self-understanding which, within the context of the sequence as a whole, provides some promise for the spring. Moving
among the dead specimens, the poet leaves the impression, after all,
of one very much alive, no longer "numb."

(10) That promise is realized in the final poem of "Heart's
Needle." Here, too, the images objectify the poet's spirits, which
have risen along with the winter wheat. Green, productive fields

take his mind's eye from the dry, sterile ground; lively colts and assertive piglets, not the snarling stuffed bobcats or the domineering stuffed lioness, surround him. Spring and the poet's daughter have both returned, and the park frees the poet from the museum.

Yet the poem is no simple vernal paean; its joy is genuine, but also reflective. As we have already noticed, the opening image of the farmer, weary in his annual accomplishments, sustains a careful balance of resignation and gratitude, responsibility and reward. The later comparison of the seasonal cycle to "merry-go-round horses" provides a similarly complex effect: the connotations are clearly positive, but such horses do go around and around all the time, firmly locked to their respective places. And while the zoo animals are old friends, they remain prisoners, and their surrender to secure care (and occasional punishment) provides admonition along with entertainment.

What is unambiguous in the poem is the simple affirmation of reunion. As the frequent use of the first-person plural pronoun suggests, the partnership of father and daughter has been reactivated: "we roast hot dogs . . . feed the swan . . . pay our respects to the peacocks." But this particular reunion, though it is by now part of a routine ("our seasons bring us back once more"), depends in the poet's eyes on far more than routine. The poet's daughter, who waved enthusiastically as she made her departure for a new home in distant Pennsylvania, has "come back." And the poet, in order to receive her, has had to stand his ground against pointed advice:

> If I loved you, they said, I'd leave
> and find my own affairs.
> Well, once again this April, we've
> come around to the bears . . . .

As both father and daughter grow older and live further apart, they must more and more *choose* their relationship. Sustaining it, season after season, against external pressures and internal tensions, must itself become an exercise in self-determination based on hard-won self-knowledge.

Spring comes again, and the whole of "Heart's Needle" comes to rest on the simplest and most modest of claims. The long chronicle—of painful separation, of good and ill portents, of self-

assertion and self-examination and self-loathing, and of a little girl
and her father hurting, strengthening, and loving each other under
hostile circumstances—ends quietly, efficiently, effectively. "And
you are still my daughter," the poet concludes. Which word must
receive the crucial emphasis? Any. All.

CHAPTER 4

An Interpolation: Remains

IN the summer of 1970, The Perishable Press published "Exactly 200 press-numbered copies" of *Remains,* a collection of eight painful, graceful poems by one "S. S. Gardons." Gardons was not entirely unknown at the time, for he had published a few poems in periodicals in the 1950s, but a note adjoining the title page provides additional information—the *only* biographical information on Gardons available anywhere, in fact. The note identifies Gardons as a Red Creek, Texas, rock musician and motorcycle entrepreneur, and it speculates briefly on his disappearance "in the mountains," an unsolved case. His friends, we learn, were responsible for collecting the sequence that appears in *Remains,* printed on handmade paper in Wisconsin, bound by hand in Cambridge, England.

There is no Red Creek, Texas.

I   *The Effort to Understand*

Gardons' collection deserves our attention here for two compelling reasons. First, it is impossible to imagine any work embodying the salutary influence of Snodgrass's best work more thoroughly than does *Remains.* The balance between intimate revelation and artistic discipline so crucial to "Heart's Needle" sustains this work as well. Indeed, as the subject of *Remains* seems in some ways even more painful than that of "Heart's Needle," its balance seems at points even more precarious and brilliant. All of the remarkable strengths of Snodgrass's personal poetry are mirrored here with neither perceptible distortion nor apparent diminution.

Second, Gardons' collection, occupied with the death of a sister and the problems and recognitions that arise as a result, raises questions precisely like ones that Snodgrass has faced and discussed himself—as in his essay, "Finding a Poem."[1] We know that, in the midst of his own effort to come to terms with the loss of his

83

daughter through divorce, Snodgrass had to face yet another sad and confounding loss, the death of his sister. She died without apparent cause, Snodgrass tells us, on a Fourth of July morning (1954) in the family home she had never chosen to leave, mourned by her parents, with whom she had always lived. She had suffered from asthma and its complications, but seemed in reasonably good health. "It would be hard to say *why* she died," Snodgrass says.[2]

It *is* hard, clearly, to say such things, but Gardons, in *Remains*, does say why his sister died: trapped in her childhood home by love and possessiveness, a victim of her own gradual surrender to continuing dependence, she allows her heart to stop beating and finds in death a means of leaving home at last. This is hard to say because it necessarily implies an indictment by Gardons of his parents as well as of his dead sister. And the task is made doubly hard by the poet's continuing, deepening love and compassion for those whom he must try to understand. But, as in Snodgrass's "Heart's Needle," Gardons must pursue the questions that loss raises, seeking, as does Snodgrass, an honest, direct confrontation with feelings so strong that they must be articulated within the discipline of art.

We may regret that the remarkable results of Gardons' courageous enterprise passed at once into rare book collections and the hands of friends, but we may reasonably suspect that the compassion that gives force to his treatment of his family may lie behind the small size of the edition, its forty dollar list price, and the present obscurity of the poet. While Gardons was not willing to compromise his statement, neither could he bear to hurt those he loves. Hence, his poems remain for the most part unknown—as does Gardons' identity.

II   *The Poems*

The organization of the volume can be described in simple terms. The first two poems, "The Mother" and "Diplomacy: The Father," provide a dramatic context for the death with which the sequence is concerned. Rival compulsions and possessive love on the one hand, a desire to cope at all costs on the other, are juxtaposed in the two portraits of the parents. The next five poems describe the young woman, the circumstances of her death, and its effects on those who "remain." Only in the final poem does Gardons break his concentration on the parental home and its sad weight. He does so in order to apply some lessons of struggle and death to a child's developing understanding of life, and he obtains thereby an effective resolution to the sequence.

(1) In "The Mother," two crucial images converge to form a fearful picture of matriarchial love, possessiveness, and self-pity. The mother is, first, *like* an aging star, in that she occupies "the dead center" of her solar system (her family) by exerting a steadily diminishing attraction on the satellites (her children) that have long shared her heat and light. But the mother is only *like* a star; her stance in the center of things is far more ominously suggestive. This simile, we discover, is subordinate to the poem's broad metaphor. In her aggressive, tenacious love, the mother is a careful spider, still striving to maintain her web:

> And the drawn strands of love, spun in her mind,
> Turn dark and cluttered, precariously hung
> With the black shapes of her mates, her sapless young,
> Where she moves by habit, hungering and blind.

The poem is one of tense juxtapositions. The mother is obsessed with the loss of her children to the "dark forces" of "the outer cold," but her sense of loss is the stable base of a secure self-pity that enables her to survive. She remains potentially destructive, but her destructiveness is finally a function of her fierce love. She has been so driven by this love that she now seems ineffectual, but in the universe she has created, her force remains palpable even to those who have escaped it. She arouses fear even as she demands pity. She is self-sufficient in her sense of righteousness, but terribly lonely. The poem is brutally frank in its depiction of the mother, but compassionate in its understanding of her compulsions. An uneasy balance, reflected in uneasy rhymes ("create it . . . hated"), suggests the ambivalence characteristic of the entire sequence and makes the portrait of the mother a formidable induction to the whole.

(2) "Diplomacy: The Father" works by a different method. It is not a description, as such, but a dramatic monologue assigned to its subject. In a Polonius-like address, the father articulates a counsel of surrender and compromise. Disengagement, cynicism, and emotional calculation are the tactics of survival that he preaches. He speaks from experience: friends must be made, for they can be useful, but their weaknesses should be observed, for these can become even more useful. In everything, one must be strategic,

alert to those moments of danger when sincerity, friendship, and generosity seem attractive. One must in such circumstances remember one's solitude in the world and maintain the balance of power that alone can protect one, a balance that is "Exactly the same / as a balance of impotence." The strategy is one of self-annihilation in the interests of survival, which is the only sure virtue in a system of absolute self-centeredness.

The obvious contrast is, of course, between the voracious force of the mother, described in the first poem, and the diplomatic submission to that force. The father's compulsion is not that of love, but of the desire to cope successfully, continually. Mother and father become greater and lesser powers in a political arena where power alone is significant, and the two together constitute and rule the world, the family, the *Remains*.

What both poems have in common is the picture of a world dangerous to its inhabitants. Strengths and talents are subject to being "bought out," trust must be refused in favor of dependence, and a sense of debt must supply the place of gratitude. Yet both poems, in the very acuity of their observation and analysis, also have in common the implied assertion of the poet's escape; he has survived the world of his family in order to obtain the critical distance from which he speaks. His sister has not.

(3) In "The Mouse," the young woman is described directly. She has been present by implication earlier, as one of those bound in the mother's web, surviving in the father's world, but her presence in the poet's memory now confirms the dramatic point of the first two poems. In her death lie the surest signs of the dangers he has intimated.

Death first enters the poem, however, through the memory of a childhood discovery. The girl and her brother, young children, find a mouse. It seems to be dead, so they bear it before them on a piece of foil. The poet recalls their weeping in the wonderful and ridiculous sensitivity of innocence.

But such innocence is doomed. Children are taught, the poem says, to be well-bred, to accept defeat as their lot, to resign their demands. And in a family governed by diplomatic concession to voracious authority, love itself will "tease" the growing child with her life. Possessive love in its full strength must have the child "just a little hurt." The image is of the mouse again, this time fallen prey to a cat that will neither kill it nor let it go.

In such a situation, there are but two alternatives. One is resignation, and the "dread" and "shock" that are its consequences.

Resignation is easy enough. It assumes the guises of unselfishness, of family loyalty, of cheerfulness even. And it can prove fatal. "Asthmatic, timid, twenty-five, unwed—" the sister dies.

The other alternative, which the poet has chosen, is escape. It is this escape, together with the knowledge it has provided, that makes him unwilling to shed at his sister's grave the tears a small mouse drew from his child's eyes. He understands too well her complicity in her own death, so will not, cannot, reflect the unconscious complicity of his parents. A sequence of poems, rather than an easy resort to graveside emotion, must stand as his complex reaction to his sister's death. And anyway, the poet had learned even as a child that there are "some things . . . Bitterer than dying."

(4) Feelings are far closer to the surface in "Viewing The Body." The banks of flowers, the flattering comments of visitors to the family, the embalmer's cosmetic arts all compel the poet to a contemptuous repudiation of the occasion. The irony is too painful to be accepted: a plain girl, by her own choice obscure and unnoticed in life, now in the coffin takes "a place of honor" in her funereal finery. And the poet, his sense of loss overmatched by his anger at the squandering of her life, will not make the polite concession and accept the irony quietly. In "Viewing The Body," he writes the most bitter poem of his career. Its final stanza is among the darkest in the language:

> Today at last she holds
> All eyes and a place of honor
> Till the obscene red folds
> Of satin close down on her.

(5) On the first anniversary of his sister's death, the poet and his young second wife return to his parents' home—to be of help at a difficult time, presumably. But the visit proves "a hideous mistake." Shadowed constantly by his sister's death, compelled to live among the remains of her life, the poet finds himself stilled, silenced, unable to help anyone. In the town, in the home, among the family that has claimed his sister, he finds himself wheezing, choking. At every turn, Gardons finds himself bound by irony and absurdity:

> It is an evil, stupid joke:
> My wife is pregnant; my sister's in her grave.
> We live in the home of the free and of the brave.
> No one would hear me, even if I spoke.

"Fourth Of July" records, in thirteen careful *abba* quatrains, the accumulation of those oppressions that lead the poet to this conclusion. It is the present tense account of a single day which joins in ghastly coincidence the anniversaries of the nation's declaration of "independence," of his sister's death, and of his wife's birthday. It is a poem steeped in the smoke of birthday cake candles and holiday skyrockets, one that justifies the growing impression of suffocation by the methodical cataloguing of precise detail.

The poet and his wife, making their visit, must be lodged in the sister's room. They fail to sleep, surrounded by objects—clothing, eyeglasses, an "asthma pipe"—which in their present uselessness recall that of the life which they once served. On the day itself, firecrackers startle the memory; they seem to mark the waste of someone who was never among "the free and the brave." And the attempt to find a distraction in a birthday celebration for the poet's wife only makes matters worse. Her vitality and earnest good cheer indict the dead for surrender. The contrast between wife and sister becomes so oppressive that the scene of celebration becomes funereal for the poet in an abstract, theatrical way, and he must abandon his meal.

The one real possibility of escape, a trip to the local park for the holiday fireworks and bands and political speeches, provides the poet with a further inspiration for dark contemplation of his sister's failure. Sitting through the crowning of the town's queen, he imagines his sister, in death, crowned a queen by those who can match her in silence and lack of feeling. She must be still in some "deprived and smoke-filled town," the poet thinks, struggling to breathe the air that she stopped breathing.

By the end of the day, as the poet and his wife and children walk home through the park, the poet's own reserves of breath grow short. He chokes in the "sulfurous smoke" of the town and wheezes in the "lint and dust" of the home. Father's world, mother's house—the poet learns again that, however strong his sense of filial obligation, he must get away in order to sustain his life. He can find nothing under these circumstances worth saying to those who want him, and even if he could, "no one would hear [him]."

(6) "Disposal" develops and extends in four carefully rhymed five-line stanzas a theme that "Fourth Of July" introduces: the futility of the sister's life becomes sadly apparent in the uselessness of the possessions she has left behind. One unused evening gown can be "fobbed off," but the rest—silver, a nightgown, the

"markdowns" she had worn—must be preserved. The process is so like burial that the obvious analogy between the things and the person who owned them cannot be avoided:

> Spared all need, all passion,
> Saved from loss, she lies boxed in satins
>
> Like a pair of party shoes
> That seemed to never find a taker;
> We send back to its maker
> A life somehow gone out of fashion
> But still too good to use.

(7) The third of the four poems that can be ascribed to Gardons' visit home one year after his sister's death is "The Survivors." As though addressing his sister, the poet adopts a reportorial tone in attempting to establish by objective evidence the effects of the girl's death upon her family. Systematically, he first surveys the yard of the family home. Then he moves inside to record, as any observer might, the behavior of the bereaved.

The yard is a panorama of neglect. No one has trimmed the lawn, weeded the rock gardens, pruned the rose bushes, repaired the trellises, or picked the fruit from the cherry tree. It is as though those responsible have grown blind to their surroundings, like the stone lions blindly guarding the front steps, their eyes patched by cement.

The appearance of the yard proves symptomatic of conditions inside the house. Here the two inhabitants, the parents, neglect not so much the things about them as each other and themselves. They move aimlessly, utterly without energy or resolve, through the dark house. They keep their distance from one another during the day and draw together at night only by a common response to the lure of the television screen. The poet hears no conversations, makes no guesses, draws no conclusions. Appearances are evidence enough of the sweeping apathy that regulates the existence in the home of the two who survive there.

The observations the poet has gathered would seem to fulfill the expectations established in the first stanza. The concrete images of a neglected yard and of neglected lives would seem to form a still life of the effects of bereavement. A sad picture, indeed. But the full depth of the family's malaise is sounded only in a couplet that concludes the poem with a startling disclosure: the signs detailed are not of change but of an enduring family condition. Although his sister's death prompted the poet to imagine changes that might take place within his family, he finds one year later that the effects of the family's loss are indiscernible. "Nothing is different here," he reports.

With "The Survivors," the poet brings to an end his analysis of his sister's death, its conditions, and its direct influence upon the sensibilities of the survivors. But there is as yet no appearance of conclusion. From the harsh, sensitive characterizations of the poet's parents to the presentation of their desolate experience as "survivors" among the "remains" of their daughter's life, the sequence of poems details more and more forcefully the poet's principal concerns: the emptiness of his sister's wasted life, the pointlessness of her death, and the complicity in which she, through her fear and apathy, joined with her loving and possessive parents. The analysis that these poems develop is thorough and persuasive, but it is, until the last poem of the sequence, essentially static, retrospective, and critical.

(8) "To A Child" effectively concludes *Remains* by striking a complex balance within the sequence and thereby conveying a sense of resolution. This poem no longer must raise and explore tough questions; it can provide gentle answers. After facing the strong realities of his sister's death, its conditions, and its consequences, the poet can share with his daughter some part of the understanding he has obtained. Having learned respect for the power of love to destroy, he can stand as a witness for the power of love to sustain.

He must do so under critical and difficult circumstances. His child, his daughter, is doubly distressed. Still trying to cope with the loss of her father and with the dislocation occasioned by divorce, she is now beset as well by fears of death. She holds on to the memory of her aunt's casket and imagines herself being placed into the ground, her own room a forfeit to someone else. These fears are further compounded by her confusion over having felt the stirrings of new life in the womb of her stepmother. Death and life have both become active mysteries for her, though she is still remarkably young. She must be taught.

The father develops his message with the poet's extraordinary care, using, as a father would, the ground of shared experiences as an oblique approach to the bare statement of simple truths. He provides, in effect, a diary of incidents and observations that intimate, for all their diversity, a growing awareness of sexuality and death, of love and hate, of creation and destruction. Father and daughter have observed lovers "napping" on riverbanks, discovered a toad run over on a graveyard road, and read the names of the dead on tombstones, the names of the living on trees. They once found a live turtle during an upstream wade and buried a dead one a week later, cheerfully agreeing, "*that* ought to make the garden fertile."

Not all of the father's attempts to share such secrets with his daughter have succeeded. He has sent her, during their separation, long letters filled with seeds and explanations of how they might be able to find nourishment for growth "far from the parent tree." Offerings of love, they failed to reach her, intercepted by those driven by less benign motives.

But such spite is less fearful and less instructive than the more dangerous threat of destructiveness under the guise of care. Father and daughter may make an effort to comprehend the forces behind the interruption of their "correspondence," but they have seen a parasitic vine strangling zinnias with "its close embrace"; they have watched men, married to embittered women, surrender their lives under the appearances of concern and consideration; they have seen an old sow fully capable of smothering or eating her own young; and they have seen a victim of love's smothering, the poet's sister, in her casket. This little child, who has already had her own difficulties in drawing breath, already knows much of death, and not a little of love. The poet states the paradox bluntly: "Without love we die; / With love we kill each other."

Having experienced both the loss of her father and the increasing possessiveness of her mother, the poet's daughter would seem to have ample excuse under the terms of this aphorism for her fears of death. Thus, the poet cannot patronize her by offering cordial platitudes, nor can he correct the impressions they have shared together.

The strategy of the poet (and of the poem) is not to correct, reinterpret, or suppress the child's knowledge of love and death, but to complete it with the good news that love can create new life. The detailed catalogue of the experience of father and child creates the necessity for and anticipates the efficacy of simple authoritative statements, with which the poem ends. Against the burden of the myriad visions of love's victims, the father throws the weight of his own example; he is one who, knowing all that the child does and

more, has affirmed the possibility of love by deliberate choice, and
he has found that choice confirmed in the new life. His authority is
the stronger for its obvious basis in experience, and the modest con-
victions he concludes with attain through careful understatement
the persuasive force of truth: "I tell you love is possible. / We have
to try."

There are few better examples in contemporary poetry of a poet's
ability to satisfy under difficult circumstances the stringent requirements of decorum. The organization of "To A Child" is both
dramatically sound in its situational bias and rhetorically coherent.
The images are vivid without seeming forced in their context, and
the diction of the poem consistently balances accuracy and con-
creteness with colloquial familiarity. Like Snodgrass, Gardons
chooses as his subject a situation clearly prone to sentimentalization.
And, again like Snodgrass, he avoids bathos by disciplining his
feelings through commitment to honesty of feeling and accuracy of
detail. Dramatic propriety in this poem, as in so many by Snodgrass,
is the direct consequence of Gardons' developing a finely balanced
correlation of speaker, occasion, and subject matter through candid
appraisal and selective organization of his own experience.

To write a sequence of blunt poems on the death of one's sister,
to indict one's parents in the process, and to conclude with a simple
statement of the need for and possibility of love, all the time
holding to the strictest artistic standards and following the most ambitious of forms, in order to produce a volume for anonymous,
restricted publication—there is in all of this a sense of a poet pursuing, with intense dedication, a style and a subject not to be
repeated, an achievement not to be equaled. *Remains* remains unique.

CHAPTER 5

After Experience

THE aphoristic simplicity of "Heart's Needle," the title Snodgrass chose for his first major poem and first collection, aptly represents the coherence and close structural unity of both the poem and the book. Similarly, the richly evocative and multifaceted title of Snodgrass's second collection, *After Experience*, provides an honest advertisement for a book of challenging diversity in both subject and style.

On the simplest level, the title indicates that the dramatized poet of Snodgrass's earlier work has now moved beyond the experiences which that work describes. More significantly, the title suggests that the characteristic point of view in the new collection will be on the whole more distant, reflective, and objective. Poems will no longer arise characteristically, as one critic described those of *Heart's Needle*, in "present tense" from "present tension."[1] The title also implies a claim for the poet as an "experienced" man. This collection draws together, or so the title would indicate, poems that are the *eventual* fruits of experience. Finally, perhaps paradoxically, the title may suggest that, while the poet is in one sense an "experienced" man, he remains intent upon—that is, "after"—continuing experience. Aesthetic distance from experience and a commitment to greater and greater relativism in its evaluation and presentation are no impediments to the poet's increasing engagement with the world. Indeed, taken as a whole, *After Experience* suggests just the opposite, that increasing objective distance from one's experience may be a prerequisite to a deeper concern for the world.

Such detailed analysis of a title is no exercise in ingenuity, for it can indicate the special character of the book. Neither a sweeping departure from the concerns and techniques of his previous work nor an exploitation of subjects and techniques already proved effective, *After Experience* is a book of consolidation, development, and

93

exploration. It cannot match *Heart's Needle* for structural coherence or dramatic intensity, but it offers a far wider range of subject and structure. It does not equal the earlier volume in consistency, but it offers a splendid opportunity to observe fruitful change and growth in the work of an increasingly resourceful and demanding poet.

And *After Experience* is in important ways a more difficult book. Most generalizations about the collection as a whole are inadequate, and first impressions of many of the poems within it tend to be unreliable. A useful caveat may lie in the striking divergence of critical opinions voiced soon after the book's publication. When one reviewer can describe *After Experience* as "an effort to sanctify the mundane by a somnambulistic rhetoric" or as "an interim book, very much concerned with its own safety,"[2] while another is able to find in it "a new richness of dialectic energy in the declaration of hostilities,"[3] then we would do well to proceed with caution. Snodgrass himself recalls the flurry of quick judgments with wry humor: "About half the reviewers beat me up because [*After Experience*] was just like my first book. The other half beat me up because it was *not* like the first book."[4]

More seasoned generalizations have followed, but these, too, can be deceptive. William Heyen finds in *After Experience* "the record of the poet's strenuous effort to order, somehow, his sense of confusion, frustration, and helplessness within some philosophical framework." The poet seeks, according to Heyen, "some truth that will enable him to live in the world as he is."[5] J. D. McClatchy quotes Heyen and paraphrases him: "In other words, the shift between books has been from awareness to understanding."[6]

The difficulty with both statements, as we shall discover, is that they are unresponsive to the complexity of the issues that the poems raise and the consciousness they develop. There may be, as Heyen suggests, some sense in these poems of a desire for philosophical system, but there is an equivalent distrust of frameworks of all kinds and little confidence that any philosophical system will prove satisfactory. At points, *After Experience* does indeed dramatize the search for truths, but one of the implicit assumptions which develops is that the notion of "some truth" awaiting discovery is unrealistic. And though McClatchy's analyses are always sound, it would be possible to argue the other side of this one formula: the speaker in *Heart's Needle* does seem, finally, to arrive at some kind of understanding, while *After Experience* represents the growth of a disillusioned awareness that renders any sense of real understanding suspect.

The point is that *After Experience* records change—in the poet, in his art, in the world—and one of the pleasures it provides is that of observing such change. The book provides us, first, with examples of Snodgrass working still very much up to form in the kind of poem he so successfully developed in *Heart's Needle*, the kind of poem to be found as well in S. S. Gardons' *Remains*. Second, it contains poems that bring the strong personal perspective implicit in "Heart's Needle" to bear upon the ambitious exploration of new subjects and different people. Third, *After Experience* in several of its poems represents genuine experimentation with new kinds of subjects and styles. In the multivoiced poems, such as "A Visitation" or "Van Gogh: 'The Starry Night,'" we are far closer in essential ways to *The Führer Bunker* than to *Heart's Needle*.

We shall find, then, that *After Experience* represents a movement from poems that deal more or less exclusively with personal experience and the self to those that deal primarily with the outside world as viewed through a personal vision. In *Heart's Needle*, when Snodgrass finds himself "walking through the universe," he characteristically concentrates on himself and the steps he takes. He celebrates, in "These Trees Stand . . . ," the illusion of his influence on nature; his principal concern is for his own experience, what it can reveal. The world is important as a mirror, for it provides the means by which the poet can learn of himself. But in *After Experience*, the poet's characteristic concern is more with the world itself. His commitment to self-understanding remains strong, but the knowledge sought in *Heart's Needle* becomes in *After Experience* a means for further exploration and analysis of the world outside.

Indeed, taken as a whole, *After Experience* portrays in brief the progress of Snodgrass's career to date. It begins with poems closely related to those of "Heart's Needle." The speaker remains the divorced father; the subject, the alienated daughter. While the distance between them has increased and seems likely to increase even further, it is clear that many of the essential concerns of the "Heart's Needle" sequence are sustained; they remain alive in the poet's mind and are still capable of drawing from him sensitive and unsparing poems. But the book concludes (excepting the translations) with five poems on Impressionist and Post-Impressionist paintings. In these poems, the attempt to dramatize an intense sympathy with works of art is conveyed through experiments with arresting image juxtapositions and with multiple voices. In between lies a fascinating record of substantial, if occasionally uneven, artistic growth.

There does remain in *After Experience*, certainly, some sense of continuity rising from implicit autobiographical references. As in *Heart's Needle*, we can discern the rough outline of the life behind the art. Yet we are less inclined to do so. One reason, as McClatchy has said, is that occasional "lyrical, depersonalized" poems in the volume break our concentration on the life of the speaker; they "serve as choric interludes by framing his experiences with more distance."[7] Another reason is that as we read through *After Experience*, the poems demand more and more of our judgment, less and less of our sympathy. Even a poem of clear personal reference, such as "A Flat One," provides no clear personal statement; alternative feelings and conclusions rest in uneasy suspension and, as a result, we are forced to weigh actively the issues which are the poem's real subject. Gradually, the persona which became so clear in "Heart's Needle" fades, and we look not so much behind, as beyond the poems of *After Experience*.

I *Saying What Has to Be Said*

Although "Heart's Needle" records unsparingly the defeats and disappointments in the poet's struggle to maintain a father's relationship with his daughter, the final impression it conveys is one of modest achievement and understanding. Father and daughter, after all, remain each other's. The long chronicle ends with them together.

After Experience, however, begins with four poems, all of which describe a new and growing distance between the two. "Heart's Needle" is informed throughout by the daughter's presence, even when she is not with the poet. But "Partial Eclipse," "September," "Reconstructions," and "The First Leaf" are all poems informed by her absence, even when they record her visits. In place of the determination to struggle against loss, which appears in so many of the poems of "Heart's Needle," there is in these four poems an equivalent sense of resignation and accommodation.

All four poems rely heavily on hard images which, as they arise from sensitive observation, frequently assume in context strong metaphoric force. In the first poem, father and daughter observe a

"Partial Eclipse" on the final evening of one of their visits. The bare details of the incident, which suggest the extent to which both allow themselves to be absorbed by the phenomenon, indicate the readiness of both to ignore for the moment the daughter's planned departure. They stand together, intent upon the slow progress of the shadow across the moon's face, sharing the common wish that the phenomenon might be as dramatic as possible. At the same time, however, the growing obscurity of the moon's face suggests how time can erase the "blackboard" of memory. Even with her by his side, the poet senses that his daughter will more and more recede from his consciousness. The loss of the moon's light anticipates his daughter's departure.

The full force of the metaphor in "Partial Eclipse" becomes apparent only in "September," when the partial eclipse has, in one sense, become total: "I can't remember / Your face or anything you said." Only a month has passed. This second eclipse, though, is one that reveals instead of concealing. Viewing the partial eclipse with his daughter and comparing it to his own reprieve from painful memories, the poet has wished the moon "all blank, bereft." Now that such eclipse has become reality, the poet's activities suggest that the obliteration of such details may not be so desirable. The poem seems addressed to the daughter, and it is clear that the poet remains imaginatively aware of her absence, that he still carries her presence with him. If "Partial Eclipse" shows the daughter's absence even in her presence, "September" signifies the opposite paradox.

Nevertheless, the poet clearly is less vulnerable. He would like to see the bird he had seen a month earlier with his daughter, but he can be casual about the bird's disappearance, too. A fine balance holds in the poem between an acute consciousness of loss and a sober sense of the limits to which one need be afflicted by it. There is no little grief in the poet's finding the face of his daughter fading into eclipse after not very much time. A sharp break in the rhyme scheme at the final sentence suggests this. But the matter-of-factness of the language tells that this grief is under control. It is part of the order in a relationship that, for the benefit of both father and daughter, must develop into a more modest and distant one.

As its title suggests, "Reconstructions" is a study of the modifications that must inevitably take place. The first three stanzas all describe attempts at independence on the part of the child, an independence projected, as is often the case with children, by a kind of intent belligerence and callousness. The poet reads in the child's natural (and in some ways healthy) meanness a model for his own assertion of independence from her. She moves in the poem from cool detachment from things she has cared for to intense possessiveness. And back again. At one point, she seems to have learned a fearful lesson from her father. She asks obedience and loyalty from the dog she has trained. When it responds, she leaves.

Although the poem projects its own attitude of cool detachment, the grief and guilt which motivate it are never far beneath the surface. The poet understands the necessity of accommodation, but he senses its costs as well. They appear in the child's cruelty to her dog, in the tedium which descends on her visits, and in the poet's awareness of her usefulness as a remunerative poetic subject. Even the poem's music—specifically, the rush of iambs and anapests in the final stanza—captures the relief the poet finds in ending his daughter's visit. And in giving her dog away.

Grief can be domesticated, it seems, and made the occasion for a kind of "play." But as the concerns of "Reconstructions" suggest, it cannot be avoided. Having committed himself to a life of choice, the poet must confront from time to time the results of his having chosen against his daughter. All may be the better for this choice, but its painful consequences continue to surface.

The most comprehensive and judicious of the four poems on the poet's continuing relationship with his daughter is "The First Leaf." The poet's ability to assume an ironic distance from his daughter's departure may seem callous at first, and the cool deliberation of his leavetaking may seem insensitive. But, as in "Reconstructions," the poet senses that his knowledge of his daughter must inevitably fade with time, just as he recognizes the extent to which his growing distance from his daughter gives him greater access to his art. Maturity can be confused with coldness, but here it should not be. In trying to choose his life, the poet recognizes that his freedom, such as it is, is in part at his child's expense. But he will not allow such knowledge to degenerate into mawkish complaint or sentimental regrets. Such would further distress the child and serve no constructive end.

The four poems at the head of *After Experience* are, then, eminently practical and sane. They are not so much remnants of the poet's former subject as a means of access to new ones. We have seen that "A Cardinal" is a kind of declaration of independence, in that the poet discovers in nature an inspiration for taking control of himself and doing his work. These four poems also constitute such a declaration, for they record the poet's sober and often painful recognition that his grasp on the daughter who so obsessed him in "Heart's Needle" must now be loosed. Time must be allowed its eraser, and the creative life, like the personal one, must expand in productivity and growth.

The two "Mementos" poems complete this statement of mature disengagement by detailing the poet's gentle adjustment to memories of his first wife. Both poems describe his responses upon discovering remnants of her presence. Like the four poems addressed to his daughter, these two, addressed formally to her mother, represent his confronting a continuing presence in his life while asserting both a growing detachment from this presence and a generous willingness that it remain.

In the first of the poems, the high school portrait of the girl who was to become his wife, the same picture he had carried with him throughout the war, reminds him of the romantic image he was able to sustain in his absence from her, one that failed to long survive the marriage. The image flourished only before they "met." Although his response to this photograph is a mixed one—it reminds him as well of the destructive struggle into which the marriage degenerated—he will not discard it. A man will not find that his past can fall into "total eclipse," even if he might wish it. And he does not.

In the second poem, other mementos provide another image of youthful romance, that of his former wife as a high school sweetheart, a reigning Queen of the May. The poet's imagination enables him to pass beyond the recent memories of a weary wife to those of a striking young woman, once his girlfriend. He will not surrender that part of his youth when his admiration for a girl sped undiminished by knowledge of the grief marriage can bring. The poem's final sentiment, expressed in its last four lines, provides as sensitive and efficient a summary of complex and painful experience as we may expect to find:

> I thought of our years; thought you
> had had enough of pain;
> thought how much grief I'd brought you;
> I wished you well again.

These two poems, "occasional" ones, ground depictions of complex mental states in the detritus of the life that has produced those states. Snodgrass thereby is able to establish as substantial those matters that otherwise would remain cloudy or sentimental.

Similarly, Snodgrass in these two poems achieves a strikingly colloquial tone that is even more forceful (the familiar paradox) because of its careful prosodic and metrical organization. In the first poem, for instance, what may appear at first as casual, if graceful, reportage is in fact the result of scrupulous construction. The first lines of each stanza establish the poem's drama in time. The long gerundial phrase that begins the first stanza by specifying the present tense of the dramatic moment is balanced by the first clause of the second stanza, which sustains the present tense even as it opens the way for a shift in the poet's frame of reference: "that first second . . . ." The opening of the third stanza makes clear its retrospective bias, just as the first line of the final stanza, by developing the crucial recognition of the third stanza, establishes a time frame for the inevitable judgment.

Or we can weigh the equal effectiveness of each stanza's final line. Each provides a statement that comprehends the substance of the preceding stanza, yet each relies on the spare, restrained language which mirrors the feeling implicit in the poem.

The second poem provides equally interesting effects, two of which deserve special attention. First, its rhyme, irregular, unobtrusive, and unforced, binds related images and ideas. With its irregular scansion and colloquial diction, the first stanza of the poem hardly seems an example of careful prosodic planning. Yet there are but five sets of rhymes in the stanza, two of which are triple rhymes. On a simple level, rhyme serves to underscore related associations, such as that between the wedding *gifts* and the dust which *sifts* to cover them, or that between the *gown* and *crown* that the girl wore when chosen "goddess of our *town*." On a more important level, however, rhyme alerts the reader to the repetitions that provide strong contrasts. Just as the brilliance of the hour in which the girl was crowned Queen of the May is compared to the dark in which the wedding gown lies packed, so are the *gown* and *crown* of her youthful office, mentioned in the first stanza, transformed finally into the *crown* of thorn and the *gown* of lead, trappings of unhappy marriage.

With the second of the "Mementos" poems, the main subject of "Heart's Needle" comes to an end. Even as they refer us back to the child, the wife, the failed marriage, the two poems establish the more distant and reflective perspective on experience that later poems will use. They are not "unfinished business."

With the poems of disengagement and accommodation behind us, we can move into the main body of *After Experience*, alert, as we should always be, to the kinds of coherence that provide principles of organization even in a collection as diverse as this one. Without undertaking systematic analysis of every poem in the collection, we can still obtain a reasonably good idea of the nature of its achievement by looking at four groups of poems: (1) five that treat with restraint and perspicacity the process of falling out of love; (2) nine that, without conveying any firm chronology, offer a series of detailed (if somewhat oblique) characterizations of the uneasy and ambiguous state of contemporary "courtship"; (3) five in which the poet more directly enters the world for his subjects, using new voices and forms in which to handle them; and (4) the remarkable five poems on paintings, discussion of which comprises Chapter Six.

II   *"The Curse Is Far From Done"*

Those poems in *After Experience* that intimate the deterioration of the poet's second marriage work largely by indirection. Unlike the poems of "Heart's Needle," which are dominated by the problems and feelings of the dramatized speaker, these seem, at least at first, far more concerned with description and analysis. Their strategies are as diverse as their subjects: a move from a year's teaching residency, the aftermath of a domestic quarrel, or the annoyance caused by a moth trapped in the bedroom at night. Nevertheless, by the time these poems reach toward the dark fear that concludes "The Platform Man," there can be little doubt as to what their essential subject has been. Together, they recount with subtle precision the inexorable decline of a working marital relationship into a threatening impasse. Far more than "Heart's Needle," which takes as its primary subject the results of a divorce, these poems, for all their attention to specific occasions and settings, constitute Snodgrass's "portrait of a marriage" and its collapse.

"Leaving Ithaca" provides a dramatic transition from the fading woes of a first marriage to the developing ones of a second by concentrating on a much more obvious kind of change, a move away from Ithaca, New York, where Snodgrass had taught for a year at Cornell. Another of Snodgrass's precariously but beautifully balanced poems, there is nothing trivial about its subject. After a year in an engagingly roughhewn house and rustic setting, the poet, forced to another move, must face the grim possibility that things have been "lovelier" than they are likely to be again. Yet he resolutely avoids taking himself or the occasion too seriously.

He chooses as his "auditor" his battered plaster reproduction of the Aphrodite of Melos, which represents for him, in a casual and offhand way, both the poet's devotion to the kind of sturdy beauty she stands for and the wear he has himself sustained (and will continue to sustain) in searching for it.

By its whimsical formality and immersion in carefully observed detail, the poem avoids any taint of the maudlin. The *abba* quatrains, despite their formal appearance, fail repeatedly to contain the poet's reflections, which take on momentum as they accumulate, independent of the formal requirements that the poem itself appears to observe. And the rhyme scheme, though it is violated only once, survives by such rhymes as "tanagers . . . managers" and "They go for the main chance . . . . They keep it in their pants."

Despite its obvious humor, though, "Leaving Ithaca" is a serious poem that conveys obliquely the outlines of a problematical and unhappy situation. The poet and his wife, expecting another child, "fume and worry," uncertain as to what their next action should be. The gravity of the situation is camouflaged by its context, for the lines in which the speaker addresses the present crisis directly are among ones given over to wry social comment on encroaching subdivisions and ones that collect in orange crates the detritus of family life.

"Leaving Ithaca" is thus a good example of the shift in method from "Heart's Needle." Instead of accepting a personal crisis as the occasion for a poem, Snodgrass depicts an occasion with such wit and in such detail that personal considerations *seem* almost tangential, a matter of casual reference. The sensitive reader should not be fooled, though he may appreciate the accumulated experience that such seasoned discretion represents.

"What We Said" at first may appear somewhat less reserved and more directly personal. The apparent pathetic fallacy in the first stanza seems to promise a poem far more thoroughly informed with the intimate concerns of the poet and his wife. And the subject itself, the aftermath of a quarrel that has shocked both, would seem to provide the opportunity for a return to Snodgrass's "confessional" mode.

It would not be surprising if Robert Phillips had had "What We Said" in mind when he criticized *After Experience* for landscapes and symbols that seem "too deliberate, too academic."[8] Clearly, most of the details in this highly detailed poem seem to derive a symbolic significance from the unhappy apprehensions of the couple observing them. And the references to "the last war" may not seem entirely convincing; their abstract intellectuality may appear arbitrary and forced in the particular dramatic context. Whatever the facts of the poet's actual experience, can the reader accept the image of the husband and wife, "stunned in that first estrangement," solemnly comparing their own problems to the record of World War II?

However problematical such matters may seem, they indicate what Snodgrass has attempted in this poem and suggest ways in which it is characteristic of his second volume of poetry. In the first stanza, by means of the obvious pathetic fallacy, Snodgrass indicates that he is not dealing with immediate experience, but describing experience on which he now has considerable perspective. As in the early poem, "Returned to Frisco, 1946," the dramatized speaker has sufficient distance from the experience he describes, so that he can dramatize not only the experience itself, but the consciousness it created.

The ghastly landscape the couple finds, with its signs of fire and neglect and abandonment, provides an objective correlative for the destructive forces the two justly fear in their marriage, even as it provides rich material for an imaginative mind's despair. The setting of the poem, then, is not so much the symbol-ridden scene upon which the couple intrudes as it is the symbol-seeking mind of the saddened husband. And while the shift from this landscape to talk of war may not seem realistic at first, this unexpected turn is the dramatic detail that reminds us of the poet's flawed, concrete individuality. The final stanza shows that the poet knows too much about the good resolutions that close the incident; perhaps he has sensed as well the staginess of the wartime comparisons. This is a poet writing "after experience."

A further indication of the poet's design may lie in the instability of his poetic medium. Despite the impression of order provided by the appearance of seven apparently well-balanced quatrains, this is a poem of calculated *dis*order. Caesurae vary so widely—in lines of uncertain rhythm—that no clear rhythmical pattern is ever established, not even as a basis for subsequent variation. Like the stuffing of a rotting couch snarled in vines, meaning spills—from line to line and, on one occasion, from one quatrain to another.

Such instability is underscored by deft handling of rhyme. *Abba* quatrains promise a certain measure of predictability, but the collection of eye rhymes ("wound . . . ground"), other slant rhymes ("woods . . . words," "lawn . . . upon"), and true rhymes that startle ("estrangement . . . change meant") hardly keeps that promise.

Both "Takeoff" and "Lying Awake" are additional examples of Snodgrass's new turn. They are still poetry of personal experience, and they are best appreciated in the implicitly biographical context in which they appear. But both poems, developing a point of view that is clearly "after experience," begin in occasion and end in aphorism. The method involves not emotion recollected in tranquillity, but relatively tranquil occasions exploited for their emotional potential.

In "Takeoff," the speaker, finding himself thirty-two thousand feet above his lover's bed, explores that peculiar sense of detachment which flight over a familiar city can bring. He can observe the city in which his woman lives, perhaps even the house in which she lies, but he is absolutely removed from her life. Love can be similarly open to the eye, but increasingly out of reach. Things soon "shrink away" as love becomes uncertain.

The uncanny sense of suspension experienced by the speaker in flight is indigenous to the poem as a whole. None of the questions raised in the poem receive clear answers. "I don't know . . . what I need to say," the speaker admits in the first stanza. By the last, he has moved only so far as a vague concession.

In "Lying Awake," the resolution is much the same: "We take things as they are." Here the speaker may be in the bed over which he has at one time flown. The poem's central image, that of a moth hurling himself compulsively around the darkened bedroom, seems to figure the speaker's own frustration. Yet the speaker holds the upper hand, for he finally cannot understand why a moth's fears of the dark compel such frantic behavior, while he has been able to survive and accommodate far darker fears inside himself.

In "The Platform Man," the poet's apprehensions, intimated in the poems that precede it, become more clearly defined: the means is the speaker's projecting a sense of nemesis onto a fearful local figure in his memories of youth. These memories, of a double amputee, a legless embodiment of deprivation and loss, still hold a dark charm over his mind; in recollected fears, he discovers a ground for his present apprehensions.

The legless man, too proud (or too cautious) to sing as he begs, proves in a way exemplary. Others who have made gains of their losses by learning compensatory skills have made themselves vulnerable to further loss, the speaker muses. To a poet who has made a new life from the wreckage of a first divorce, the lesson should be clear. The "platform man" ran no such danger, as the speaker remembers him, for his loss was for him "bad enough / Without more things to lose." Even before the final three lines of the poem, the application of this memory to the speaker's own situation has become ominously clear. But unlike the "platform man," he has not learned from one loss how to protect himself from a second:

> The curse is far from done
> When they've taken your daughter;
> They can take your son.

In five poems, we have come a long way through the deterioration of the speaker's relationship with his wife. From the shock of "first estrangement" we have moved in short order to the speaker's fears that he stands to lose yet another child.

III   *Interim Poems: "Tuned and Under Tension"*

Before we examine the several most important and innovative poems in *After Experience,* those that most dramatically reveal Snodgrass's changing means and ends, we should look at one further informal grouping of poems that precedes them. Though they provide little reliable sense of chronology, the ten poems from "Looking" to "Regraduating the Lute" are related to one another by common thematic concerns. In this series, which as a whole offers an oblique characterization of the plight of modern man between loves, we find a rich and diverse mixture of straightforward revelations, acute observation, anecdotal reflection, even a bit of artful posturing. The poems are not "confessional," for they do not insist upon the poet's intense personal involvement. But they are poems of personal experience, even though the experiences involved do not demand the kind of thorough self-revelation prompted by those revealed in earlier poems. A "needle" remains, but it seems not so close to the poet's heart.

These poems describe a kind of hiatus in the search for love. Ap-

propriately so, for they are poems that reveal the practiced, graceful
application of techniques already proven under more exacting circumstances. For all of their undeniable virtues, the poems seem interim works, successful and unstartling lyrics that take the reader
from poems closely allied to the "confessional" impulse to the distinguished segregate works that conclude the first part of the
volume.

"Looking" and "Autumn Scene" both establish, in Snodgrass's
careful way, an observation on directionless, unproductive behavior.
The first is immediately personal. The speaker describes a day in his
own experience, one of distraction and uncertainty; he becomes in
his own memory a man much like the threatened, forgetful subject
of Frost's "An Old Man on a Winter Night." But age is not this
speaker's problem. The poem reveals too much intelligent self-
consciousness for that. Rather, as the rocking, incantatory rhythm of
the lines suggests, the feeling is one of daze, stupor and indeter-
mination.

Although the events described are those that take place through
the course of a single dreary day, the primary subject of the poem is
the speaker's inability to account for his day. The questions he
raises receive no answers. The one judgment he makes
("Everywhere I was, was wrong") seems forced, more a symptom
than a resolution. In the conjunctions that provide the thread for
the heart's meandering (the third stanza), we can read the laziness
of mind that is the crucial issue.

The same mood is reexamined in "Autumn Scene." The implied
judgment against the point of view developed in the poem is that
this point of view can itself produce no judgment. The account of
the people out walking is as cool and austere as the people
themselves seem to be. Pathetic fallacy in the first stanza and simile
in the fourth fall flat, for they seem to be the products of a wit never
engaged. Whatever knowledge animates the observation never
becomes apparent. As in "Looking," the poem portrays the
workmanlike operation of a weary and disengaged intellect; indeed
it is one glimpse in a day of "looking."

In the next five poems, the ennui suggested by "Looking" and
"Autumn Scene" becomes charged with lies, adultery, concessions,
and admissions. We hear the desperate voice of a man searching for
love among the deceptive lures of contemporary society. The
strongest passions are discredited by the banality of the circumstances that surround them, the struggles that develop seem ig-

noble, and the sacrifices that must be made seem weary surrenders to the inevitable. In these five poems love (or its appearance) seems discredited, a leveling and mediocre instinct. Whatever the relation of this "adultery group" to Snodgrass's own hard times between his second and third marriages, it represents a harsh but just dramatization of contemporary social malaise.

The virtues of these poems are many: their language is often strikingly colloquial, their portrayal of widely varying feelings rings true, and their images ("is the second bed / Unrumpled . . .") prove startlingly just. But if these poems are measured against the standard of "Heart's Needle," according to "the depth of their sincerity," they fall far short. The fragile balance in the earlier cycle between intimate revelation and subtle artistic control is replaced by a workmanlike junction of dramatized revelation and conspicuous control, the means of which are far more obvious.

For instance, in both "No Use" and "That Time," spontaneity and candor are suggested not by the poet's unstated, inescapable engagement with his subject, but by several manifest linguistic devices, among them ellipsis. Or, in "A Friend," the device used is a strong contrast between levels of diction: the speaker first provides himself with a vainglorious nickname, then descends to rank vulgarity in describing a drive-in theater. Such devices display the poet's resourcefulness and skill even as, by their prominence, they tend to inhibit the reader's sympathy with him.

Snodgrass may well intend this response, of course. In the dramatic context of the series in which these poems lie, their banality, unsignifying cleverness, mixed metaphor, and prosy reportage weigh primarily against the character of the dramatized speaker, which seems further and further removed from that of the poet. We have observed Snodgrass declaring his independence in other ways at other times, but in these poems he begins most clearly to reassert his distance from the "I" of the speaker in the poem. The extent to which the poems are or are not autobiographical is not nearly so significant as the fact that they fail to obtain and exploit the kind of authority so essential to the depth of meaning in "Heart's Needle" and other of Snodgrass's highly personal poems.

It is not an easy matter to discriminate, using wholly objective tools, between the kind of tension achieved in "Heart's Needle," where both honesty and artistic control seem hard won and extraordinary, and that in these poems, where both artistry and the impression of candor seem practiced and deliberate. "Confessional" poetry convinces us that it does not represent simply one artistic alternative freely chosen from among the many available, but the only possible means of expression for the poet at the time. And we have already explored the extent to which this conviction informs our appreciation of a poem's method and meaning. But in the poems of the "adultery group," what we sense instead is precisely the poet's skillful choice among expressive strategies. The question of autobiographical content seems not particularly pertinent, for we are not convinced that the poet was compelled to these poems by his experience. We recognize that the poet may have drawn upon his experience for his poems, but that is a different matter entirely.

In "Regraduating the Lute," Snodgrass himself provides the most persuasive support for such distinctions. Here, as in the earlier, more immediately personal poems, the subject is a modest, domestic one, minutely observed and meticulously reported. There is little obvious wit, no patent structural cleverness, and no conspicuous shift in tone. Instead, we have a lutenist's description of the process by which he makes his instrument his own. It is because the poem is so faithful to its own announced design as the expert chronicle of a loving task that it can become something else as well—a sustained symbolic statement of commitment to a new love. The entire success of the symbol of the lute makes possible the significance of the final detail. It is at once an admission of the instrument's symbolic status in the poet's life and the final step in the process of search he has described.

IV   "Justice of Vision": Five Poems

"*Is* that the way the world is? *Is* that the way I experience the world?" These questions have always occupied Snodgrass, but as his poetry becomes more concerned with the world itself, they become more prominent. Snodgrass recalls an introduction he once read to the *Iliad*, in which the writer speaks of Homer's having made "a vocation of justice of vision." The paraphrase is apt, for as Snodgrass turns progressively from using his own experience as the primary subject of his poetry, to the world itself, his intent to "make his vision just" becomes more and more crucial. While we might follow Snodgrass's suggestion in evaluating his "confessional" poems according to "the depth of their sincerity," we become much more concerned in his later poems with the impression of authenticity they provide. "Does it *feel* authentic? Does it *feel* like the way the world feels?"[9]

These questions will be especially crucial in considering the poems on paintings and those of *The Führer Bunker*. But they apply as well to the important poems in *After Experience* that lead us still further from the poetry of personal experience as they anticipate the moral relativism, stylistic experimentation, and "authentic" reportage of the later works.

The five poems we shall consider, despite their remarkable diversity of style and subject, manifest a common interest in realities that await discovery behind appearances. They are, moreover, all poems of movement, in one sense or another; they enact, to a greater extent than any of Snodgrass's earlier works, his professed intention to write poems in which time passes and people and ideas change. They all suggest Snodgrass's interest in going beyond the rigid forms of his personal poems to experiment with informal (though hardly undisciplined) structures.

Finally, they all reveal a poet beginning "to be as relativistic as possible" in the morality indigenous to his works. From the poems on paintings through those of *The Führer Bunker*, Snodgrass forces his readers to question their conventional beliefs about right and wrong. He imposes upon them the responsibility of judging among alternative attitudes and points of view. He creates the poem as (among other things) "an act of aggression against the reader's narrow definition of himself and what he believes and what he thinks."[10]

The changes in design and achievement that appear in these later poems are more striking there, as we shall see. But they begin to become clearly apparent, and highly important, in the poems like "A Flat One," "The Men's Room in the College Chapel," "Planting a Magnolia," "A Visitation," and the title poem, "After Experience Taught Me . . . ."

Of these five poems, "A Flat One" seems most familiar in subject and style. The experience it details is autobiographical: its title, hospital slang for a corpse, refers specifically to Fritz Jarck, the "old man who was dying" mentioned in "April Inventory." Snodgrass cared for the World War I veteran as part of his orderly's duties at a Veterans Administration hospital. He began work on the poem while he was still in Iowa; and as in most of his poems based on personal experience, he chooses a tight stanzaic form. But we must not overestimate the poem's affinities to Snodgrass's earlier work.

Although its roots are in Iowa and its structure is formal, "A Flat One" belongs in more important ways to the poems among which it stands. It is one of the clearest illustrations of the pursuit of "justice

of vision" in Snodgrass's poetry. Its speaker already knows the falsity of easy moralizing ("a worthwhile job"). But he must discover as
well the falsity of easy cynicism before he can move through his opposed feelings to a hard-won admission, a just vision of a small reality behind large and conflicting appearances.

The poem expresses as well Snodgrass's concern with relativism.
Alternative attitudes and feelings arise during the poem, and they
neither cancel one another nor become reconciled. The hospital
orderly's relief at the end of a tedious and unrewarding assignment
is as credible as his barely concealed admiration and affection for
his patient. His gruff and impersonal efficiency in working on the
corpse is convincing, but so is the familiarity he adopts in addressing it. We can discount neither the speaker's admiration for
Jarck's determination to live at all costs, nor his disgust that such
determination brings only futile suffering. The poem sustains a
moving argument against a hospital's power to "torment" a dying
man "to life," yet it closes with the speaker's fierce admission that
the man's perverse insistence on living has demanded and deserved
from him loyal, unthinking devotion.

In reading the poem, we must confront and weigh these attitudes, but we are supplied no easy choices among them. Like the
dramatized speaker, we must be active in seeking something to af-
firm among the contrary truths of a complex dilemma. In other
words, we face "an act of aggression" against our belief that there
must be a "proper" response to such problems. The poem shows the
world as it is, not as the poet would like it to be.

But it is not only in the complex of the poem's attitudes that
Snodgrass achieves the relativism that jars his reader into action.
The primary source of the poem's relativism is its language. We can
get some idea of the poem's subtlety and depth by observing just
three of the most important phenomena in it.

The first is verbal ambiguity—not lack of clarity but intended
multiple meaning. The first stanza provides two good examples.
The seven months of mortal illness for "Old Fritz" have been
wasted months in several senses. The hospital orderly thinks them
squandered on a hopeless case; neither he nor his dead patient has
derived any return from all of the suffering and effort. In another
sense, the months have been actively consumed, worn away by the
routine of care and by the ebbs and flows of pain. Finally, they have
been months spent upon a patient *wasted* by illness. We transfer the
adjective unconsciously, sensing the implicit epithet.

The adjective *unfit* is similarly rich. The patient is remembered as unable to move because of his illness; his body would not fit him for the task. He was also, in some sense, unworthy for movement, "no good to yourself or anyone. . . ." Nor, "shrunken, gray," was he a fit object for being moved, though the speaker and the other orderlies were charged with moving him daily.

Such examples abound. "Seven months *gone down the drain*" would seem the usual cliché, were the corpse being addressed not also being drained on the morgue's steel table. The "*deadening drug*" is analgesic, yet we have learned that it can prove fatal, as well. "Time, drugs, and . . . minds" have been spent on Fritz Jarck to keep him "hanging on": not only surviving, from day to day, but "tormented . . . / To life" on "Dark Age machinery."

Oblique, multifaceted allusions are also part of the poem's relativism. Eucharistic and sacrificial references in stanzas four and sixteen are good examples. For the orderly, memories of feeding time prompt sacramental associations. By means of "pious sacrifice," of time and resources, the patient was given enough strength to endure still more pain. Administration of body (haddock's) and blood (tomato's) provided new life for him daily. But just as the elements of feeding parody those of the Christian Eucharist ("Receive this . . . body, . . . take this blood . . ."), so is the life that the patient receives a parody of the spiritual restoration promised by the traditional Eucharistic meal. And in addition to being a "communicant" in a bleak, nonrestorative sacrificial meal, "Old Fritz" also hangs, in the orderly's mind, as a kind of sacrificial victim. He remembers his patient as "Nailed to . . . rapacious, stiff self-will," a doomed man crucified by his own determination to live. The poem's ironic religious allusions are integral to its relativism because we must measure the variable distance between the primary reference (e.g., Jarck's suffering) and the association it prompts (i.e., crucifixion). By judging the relative propriety of the allusions, we define and in part create the poem.

Finally, sharp shifts in syntax throughout the poem alert us to constant shifts in the nature of its point of view. The poem begins with four stanzas of retrospective chronicle, broken only by the speaker's quoting himself ironically in the fourth. In the fifth through the ninth stanzas, the remembered patient, more and more objectified by the account of his care, becomes pure object, a corpse. Through the next seven stanzas, analysis again concentrates on the past, rendered this time, however, in past perfect tense—our concern shifts from what the orderly has done or must do to the subject himself and the issues raised by his agonizing decline. Having been reduced from patient to corpse, "Old Fritz" is rejuvenated in the poem by the record of his grim, blind courage. The poem's final shift comes in the last two stanzas, when the speaker attempts one kind of conclusion—"We kept / You, because we need to earn our pay"—but must settle for another: "No. We'd still have to help you try. We would / Have killed for you today."

These shifts in tense and focus should remind us that "A Flat One" is not about a corpse, but about the effort of an active and sensitive mind to work out a reasonable and defensible response to a moral enigma. We are less concerned, finally, with the poet's experience than with his mind, its flexibility before a wide range of answers, and its final immunity to easy answers of cynics and idealists. The poem provides no good answers because there are none that seem to ring true in the world as it is. That is the way the world feels.

"The Men's Room in the College Chapel" is another attempt to get at "how things really are"—and always have been. Strongly place-centered, the poem is a meditation on the bestial forces in the human soul. Above the speaker's head lies a Christian chapel, with its trappings of civilized piety. But he is moved to contemplate the true nature of man's soul by the lewd and scatological scribblings he finds in the toilet. The irony that the poem develops is, simply, that this evidence of man's "old, lewd defiance" is also evidence of his humanity, signs that finally testify in favor of the species.

The poem begins by constituting its place, a traditional meditative device. A more superficial poetic imagination might rest content in observing the chapel's metaphoric representation of Christian dualism—spirit above, body below. But here, it is within the "four gray walls" of the toilet stall that Snodgrass finds the whole man, his spirit revealed in his crude obsessions with bodily functions. Such is man's nature, just as it is his nature to throw up camouflage. Hence, the stanza's final line points in two directions, for the poem's subject is not only man's defiance of abstract notions of decorum. In a real sense, man defies mankind. Men climb beneath the pious trappings of religious ceremony that they have themselves erected, so that they can defy and assert themselves simultaneously.

The following two stanzas detail historical associations that develop in positive ways the poet's view of those instincts he has found revealed. The gray walls of the stall remind him first of a prisoner's compulsion, however desperate his plight and futile his chances of communication, to "carve his platform in the walls." Both the totemic drawings of cave men and the faithful inscriptions of Christian catacombs signify man's indomitable need to carve himself and his beliefs upon public walls—no more and no less than the men's room drawings that lie before the poet's eyes.

Man's soul must find its cave, the last stanza tells us, where it can turn "like a beast / nursing its wounds" to gather strength and resolve on action. Strength for what? Here the relativism of this poem becomes clear. Like the men's room drawings, the poem itself speaks of the way man's soul is, not of the way we might wish it to be. The poem represents; it does not judge. From the urgings that Snodgrass finds exemplified in the men's room may rise noble statements of faith or defiance. But such urgings may also produce the mutterings of a Fegelein or the compulsive ambitions of a Hitler.

"Planting a Magnolia" works by a similar method, as the poet again searches behind appearances for realities pertinent to what he observes. In some sense, the poem's essential subject seems not to be "planting a magnolia," but the contrast in man's mind between his deceptive sense of control over nature in all its forms and the lesson brought by the tree—man's essential triviality before nature and his subjection to its irresistible force.

This fundamental contrast, which represents the accumulated meaning of the poem, rests on a number of more restricted contrasts that develop as its associations proliferate. One is that between the domestic pleasure appropriate to taking delivery and the sinister associations attached to the process of planting. The tree seems a fox's prey, destined for its grave. In spring, the tree will be beautiful—if it survives. But the flowers, "white as flakburst," will seem, as they develop from "lewd buds" upon "serpent boughs," cancer cells. At the height of its soft beauty, the magnolia tree will still intimate a kind of threat. A complex of contrasts, the tree will remain throughout its life a source of beauty both pleasing and fearful.

The source of this imagined threat is twofold. The tree's deep ancestral memories indict the petty possessiveness of those who have ordered and planted it. "It stands . . . waiting / To declare itself" in the present moment of the poem, a potential of bud and flower and leaf that its new owners look forward to. But its roots lie deep in death: in the "ripe leaf rot" of its mulch and in "the Age of the Great Dying," when all of "its old / Familiars . . . Perished with their successes and were gone." Against this record of knowledge and endurance, the presumptions of its new owners stand revealed as absurd and arrogant.

But there is a crucial sense, as well, in which the magnolia mocks the presumptions of all men, of mankind. The poem arises from a particular incident, but it opens, toward the end, into a far more general statement. The speaker becomes, as the plural pronouns suggest, a representative of the species. Man attempts to force nature to his uses. If skillful, he can enjoy it for a time. But the magnolia is, above all, a survivor; and man, above all, is not. The beauty that surrounds man will survive him, and the tree's dark intimations of cold and death will become his reality.

The poem begins by recognizing and announcing "a mystery." It concludes with a terse statement of that mystery. The associations that develop in between, fruits of an energetic, deeply serious mind, are dominated throughout by the brooding presence of the dormant tree. Nevertheless, the voice remains that of the poet. If the tree is to speak at all, it will await spring. We no longer can feel safe in calling the speaker "Snodgrass," but neither are we forced yet to admit the speaker's virtual independence from the poet. Such an admission would take us even further into relativism and require our judgment to a far greater degree.

That admission is required by "A Visitation" and "After Experience Taught Me. . . ." We hear voices that cannot belong to the poet, voices that contend with the dramatized poet's or with each other as they assume particular dramatic identities of their own. And the result is that, more than at any time previously in Snodgrass's poetry, we are called upon to weigh critically all that we hear, to judge where judgment is possible, and to avoid judgment when it would be unrealistic or inappropriate (responsibilities that will become even more critical in *The Führer Bunker*).

The question of judgment might at first seem moot in "A Visitation," for the "visitor" is the ghost of Adolf Eichmann. As the headnote from Hannah Arendt reminds us, no man has ever been condemned more universally or more confidently. His crimes against humanity seemed radical aberrations from human nature itself, unmeasurable by any rational criminal code. The human race, Arendt's statement suggests, rose to cast Eichmann out, unwilling "to share the earth" with a monster.

But it is not Eichmann we are called upon to judge during the course of the poem, though we should be alert to the extent to which his cunning arguments are self-serving. Nor are we asked to judge the poet, who finds the executed Eichmann "turned . . . loose" upon his conscience. We are asked, by the terms of the dramatic exchange between the two, to judge ourselves.

The ghost's argument is simple. Unlucky enough to be in the wrong place at the wrong time, he became, he says, a scapegoat for man's fears of his own deceit and violence and greed. His crime, though real enough, was a matter of "Luck . . . not character." Like some wheedling salesman, the ghost seeks admittance on the grounds that he and the poet have played the same game, taking "the parts / Our time and place allowed." The ghost of the man who was only following orders reminds the poet, "You've chained men to a steel beam on command." He says, in effect, you're different from me not because you're better, but because you're luckier.[11]

The poet, for his part, is willing to concede some part of the ghost's argument. He has followed orders, though not "on so grand / A scale." But he will not admit to the essential crime of Eichmann,

> the abstract
> Gray lie, the sweet cliché that still imparts
> Its drugged glow through the brain.

The poet knows, or is making an attempt to know, his share of deceit and violence and greed. The ghost counterattacks effectively, however, by shifting the frame of reference from warfare to domestic life. In question after question, he probes for the poet's own experience of self-deceit, for the "deep faults" that require only the proper circumstances to rise to the surface.

For all his clever argument, the ghost does not quite prevail. His "crime," philosophy, keeps him on the sill. Or does it? "How subtle all that chokes us with disgust / Moves in implacably to rule us, un-aware." At last, the ghost would seem to have won the point. "Watch the way your world moves," he tells the poet; "you can look through me."

How do we read the pun? Do we concede the poet's defeat, his subjugation to the ghost of Eichmann? No, but we may recognize its possibility. What we judge most strictly by the experience of this

poem is overconfidence of judgment arising from simplistic op-
timism about human nature. Speaking of the despicable Nazi, Hermann Fegelein, Snodgrass
once admitted:

If Fegelein were here, and I had a revolver, I know what I would do. But
that doesn't absolutely guarantee that if I had been raised in his place at
that time, under those conditons, that I would have resisted those things he
didn't resist. I can't be absolutely positive, though I *hope* so. I hope I am
different. To admit that you're not much better than the man you're killing
is a pretty fearful thing. But there is a strong possibility that it is true.[12]

And in this deft *terza rima,* Snodgrass gives dramatic form to the
"pretty fearful thing" that is so difficult to admit. The only thing
more fearful, as *The Führer Bunker* makes clear, is willful ig-
norance. The man most capable of becoming another Eichmann is
the one who can find no part of Eichmann in himself, who cannot
recognize Eichmann as a member of the human race.

We are fortunate that the painful ambiguity of this strong and
sensitive poem is more broadly detailed, if not resolved, in the title
poem of the volume. "After Experience Taught Me . . ." is
another juxtaposition of distinct voices on the essential sources of
human action, another attempt to approximate as justly as possible
the way things really are. But its method is different in obvious
ways. The voice of the dramatized poet does not appear until the
final conclusive stanza; the poet learns from, but is not a party to,
the exchange that takes place. And the tension that seems to spring
up from the juxtaposition of the two voices in this poem is more apparent than real; part of the poem's method is to enable us to discover a common affirmation in statements radically dissimilar in
style and context. The stakes in "After Experience Taught
Me . . ." may not be as high as those in "A Visitation," but what
the poem lacks in dramatic force it makes up in the breadth of its
reference to the concerns of the volume as a whole.

The two voices are those of Spinoza, the seventeenth-century
Dutch philosopher, and of an instructor in hand-to-hand combat.
Spinoza's lines, flush left in the poem, come from the first
paragraph of his *Treatise on the Correction of the Understanding*
and from Propositions XXII and XXI in Part IV of *The Ethics,* "On
Human Servitude, or the Strength of the Emotions." The military
instructor's lines are presumably drawn from Snodgrass's memory
of his own training. Neither's remarks require much elucidation.

Spinoza announces his search for "something truly good and able to communicate its goodness" at the opening of his treatise.[13] Were we to continue, we would discover that the end of Spinoza's search is intended to be the application of all knowledge, all the sciences, to the attainment of "the greatest possible human perfection."[14] But instead of using these lines, Snodgrass juxtaposes two propositions that assert the virtue of highest priority—self-preservation. There is no philosophical inconsistency here, of course; man must "actually exist" before he can entertain any higher aspirations. But Snodgrass makes his point, nevertheless. Whatever a man may think his ultimate concern to be, his essential prior concern is "to be, to act, to live."

And it is to this end that the combat instructor, whose lines are indented, speaks. His concerns are entirely practical. He demonstrates how a soldier, facing close combat with no weapon, can employ "something very / Ugly" to save his life. Given sufficient skill and strength, he can "rip off" his enemy's face, taking his life and his identity from him simultaneously.

In one sense, the drill instructor's lines merely illustrate the Dutch philosopher's fundamental recognition. But as its final quatrain makes clear, the poem is more than a clever exposition of the reality of human nature. After listening to philosopher and combat instructor, disembodied in their artfully balanced counterpoint, we hear the direct passionate voice of the poet, accusing himself and us:

> And you, whiner, who wastes your time
> Dawdling over the remorseless earth,
> What evil, what unspeakable crime
> Have you made your life worth?

This is not simply another reminder of the familiar principle that life, on whatever level, depends on victory and is sustained by deaths. Nor is it safely hyperbolic, an isolated reference to the kinds of extreme behavior considered in *The Führer Bunker*.

At the end of the title poem of *After Experience*, we need look no further than "Heart's Needle" for the most poignant illustration of its principle. That poem details in painful candor the extent to which a man's exercise of choice must often hurt deeply those whom he most loves.

And in the fourth poem of *After Experience*, "The First Leaf," that recognition arises once again as the poet-father considers his

separation from his daughter: "This year you will live at our expense; / We have a life at yours." It is a recognition never far
removed from the poems of the volume. In order "to actually exist," a man must have the courage and the strength to choose his
life. But in making his choices, he must recognize two critical principles. One is that choosing "to be, to act, to live" often requires
choosing to hurt; that is the lesson of "Heart's Needle" and of
much of *After Experience.* The other is that, while he must attempt
to be responsible in and for his choices, he must never succumb to
the illusion that he is entirely free in them; that is part of the lesson
in "Van Gogh: 'The Starry Night,' " for instance, and in the poems
of *The Führer Bunker.*

CHAPTER 6

Poems at an Exhibition

WITH the five poems on late nineteenth- and early twentieth-century paintings, Snodgrass's concern with the diversification of his achievement becomes even more apparent. The poems are in one sense experiments, the result of the poet's deliberate attempt to explore the range of his talent by treating specific works of art in depth. In another sense, though, as we shall see, they are finished works that reflect Snodgrass's increasing resourcefulness and maturity.

Snodgrass is not the only modern poet to have written on paintings—others include William Carlos Williams ("Pictures from Brueghel"), W. H. Auden ("Musée des Beaux Arts"), Anne Sexton ("Starry Night"), and Irving Feldman ("Portrait de Femme")—but he may well be the most ambitious. The implicit claim of every poem on a work of art is that the poet, through careful observation of his subject, has achieved a particular communicable response to it, found a revealing rationale for evaluating its success, or formed a strategy for re-creating some of its effects through words. Snodgrass's particular claim in this curious subgenre is that he has sought to reach all three of these ends in every poem—for the most part, successfully.

I *The Occasion of Transition*

Curiously, Snodgrass's impetus to attempt poems about paintings was supplied by false promises. An art magazine proposed that he write a poem on some major work of art, only to withdraw its offer later. That the magazine reneged is, happily, incidental, for Snodgrass found the assignment so attractive that his satisfaction with one such poem led him eventually to four others.

Admittedly, the question of Snodgrass's apparent qualifications for such an enterprise raises a paradox. At the time of the

119

magazine's invitation, Snodgrass had had little formal experience in the interpretation of art. He had once taught a single session of a short-lived course in modern art, but only after insisting that he knew nothing about the subject. And the interpretative methods he describes in his essay, "Poems About Paintings," are ones that even a beginning art student should mistrust: he can join free association, arbitrary biographical speculation, and eclectic patching together of far-removed theories and recollections in utter disregard for prevailing professional opinion (RP, pp. 64 - 69).[1]

But Snodgrass has no intention of contributing to the history of art. His claim in these poems is not for an educated eye, but for a sensitive, naive, and unprejudiced one. He proposes not so much to analyze a made object as to make an object himself. His first obligation is not to someone else's painting, but to his own poem. A seeming liability, then, the lack of expertise in the interpretation of art, may paradoxically be one of Snodgrass's claimed assets in these poems.

Another apparent paradox emerges from Snodgrass's admission that he completed the poem on Matisse's "The Red Studio" with unexpected ease. The experience was both heartening and misleading. Choosing the next painting, for instance, proved difficult, and each poem, as we shall see, would pose distinctive problems of its own. The paradox lies not in Snodgrass's frustrated expectations of easy poems, however, but in his delighted discovery that difficult, complex, highly intellectual poems can prove far kinder to a poet than more direct poems in a "confessional" mode. The recognition is important to many of the poems of *After Experience*, but especially so to the poems on paintings.

Two major dangers confront the "confessional" poet who tries to mine a finite vein of personal experience ever and ever deeper, and both are amply illustrated in the tragic history of contemporary poetry. One is preciosity, the attempt to refine profound meaning from trivial experience. The more frightening danger is that of being consumed by the compulsion to force self-knowledge and self-revelation to further and further limits. It may be improperly inferential to assume that Snodgrass saw such dangers in his own path, but we may surmise that he discovered in poems about paintings a form that, by requiring some measure of personal detachment on the part of the poet, can provide considerable safety from both preciosity and psychological crisis.

But poems that represent growth in Snodgrass, not a temporary peregrination in the career of a "confessional" poet, deserve a more positive approach. One such approach has been suggested by Richard Howard and Jerome Mazzaro. While the two fail to agree on the merits of the poems about paintings, both find them attempts on Snodgrass's part to manifest personal as well as artistic growth. Howard, who finds that Snodgrass's "confessional" poetry portrays stages in the "unification of the self," believes the poems about paintings may intimate the fruition of that process. They reveal a poet who "no longer needs to double himself . . . in order to create himself."[2] Mazzaro thinks that what growth can be perceived in the "painting" poems is "a growth without any real resistance . . . a growth in a masturbatory rather than real world." But even to him they seem an assertion by the poet of his "continuing evolution and freedom," or, at least, of his need to prove it.[3] These assumptions regarding Snodgrass's personal psychological advances may not be very helpful, but they can point us to distinctive qualities in the poems which may have inspired them.

One is the authority the poems assert in developing what are, after all, highly distinctive responses to well-known works of art. These responses, far more than the paintings, inform the poems. The poet's active intelligence does not simply follow the painter's hand, but penetrates beyond it, even in apparent defiance at some points of the painter's intentions. So in these poems ostensibly based on and thus limited by particular works of art, we obtain a strong sense of the poet's authority.

The other quality deserving notice is closely related: it is the consistency with which this authority is applied to effect, in Snodgrass's words, the "transformation of matter into energy" (*RP*, p. 76). Had Snodgrass chosen paintings that convey a highly dramatic and clearly articulated force, his authority would not be so apparent. But Snodgrass has chosen paintings that reveal a dramatic situation only under the pressure of the poet's eye. For instance, instead of Picasso's highly emotional "Guernica," which immediately confronts the visitor to the Museum of Modern Art, Snodgrass chose Monet's "Les Nymphéas," which hangs quietly in another room, offering seeming loveliness and placidity to gazers, intensity only to those who are willing to seek its accumulative forcefulness.

The paintings Snodgrass has chosen await (or, Snodgrass might say, contain) a process of transformation. The matter of art must become the energy of viewed art. It is this process, both imposed and discerned by the poet, that makes apparent his authority and

freedom. And it is this process as the poet dramatizes it in each
poem that makes of the five poems a series that finally conveys an
impression greater than the sum of its parts. Our impression is one
not so much of "poems about paintings," as one of poems about the
experience of observing paintings and making them our own.

II "The Red Studio"

If Snodgrass had not warned us, we would be justified in assuming his "choice" of the Matisse painting to be deliberate. How
better for a "confessional" poet to effect a transition in poetry than
by choosing a work by the strongest proponent of sincerity in painting? Matisse's emphatic call still resounds: "I cannot stress enough
the absolute necessity for an artist to have perfect sincerity in his
work, which alone can give him the great courage he needs in order
to accept it in all modesty and humility."[4]
    The words easily could be Snodgrass's own. Moreover, the choice
of "The Red Studio" would be apt also because the painting
signifies questions present in all of the poems about paintings, ones
concerning the representation of a second creation. For the first of
his poems about paintings, Snodgrass takes up the most famous of
paintings about paintings. Jean Guichard-Meili, curator of the
Bibliothèque Nationale, Paris, sees in this painting "a means of
suggesting, in a new form, a certain ambiguity of reality, a cleverly
calculated uncertainty between the thing or person and its image . . . ." In this way, Guichard-Meili says, "Matisse showed that
things are unattached and easily slip from reality into the world of
painting and *vice-versa*."[5] This possibility of slippage, as we shall
see, becomes a dominant theme in Snodgrass's poem.
    However, while these considerations enhance our appreciation of
how well suited the painting is to Snodgrass's purposes, they apparently did not determine his choice. The source of the poem, according to Snodgrass, lies in that single art appreciation class he
taught. "The Red Studio" was the second slide screened for the
evening's discussion, and the responses to it that developed, both
among the students and in Snodgrass's own mind, provided the impetus for beginning the poem. These circumstances are interesting
because they suggest the basis of Snodgrass's poem in active, naive
responses to the work of art. When "The Red Studio" popped up, it
aroused no questions of influence or chronology. These were
probably answered by Snodgrass's teaching kit. Rather, it provoked

Snodgrass to find it "quite gay, lively, energetic," even as it impressed one of his students as "absolutely terrifying."

The disparity between these two reactions—both highly subjective—provided Snodgrass with a point of departure; he began to try to determine how both might be right. The route of free association Snodgrass followed in this pursuit was far-ranging, from a psychiatrist's rug to childhood nightmares, from Dante to carnival rides, from ancient theories of the universe to contemporary ones.

All that remained was a dramatic occasion capable of fulfilling, if not of accommodating, such varied analogues. This he developed by working on an explanation for the "strange, almost inhuman quality" of the painting. What has happened, he decides, is that the artist has sacrificed himself, exploded his own matter in order to provide the new forms and intense energy present in the painting. The only evidence of this sacrifice is the impression of emptiness, of open space, at the painting's center, but that is enough.

So both Snodgrass and his pupil are right. If the studio's gaiety and energy testify to the artist's obliteration, admiration and terror are both appropriate responses.

The poem that is the expression of this discovery is not so reticular as the process that produced it. "Matisse: 'The Red Studio' " manages to contain the poet's associations, but it does so within the context of a hypothetical dramatic situation that dominates and orders the whole.

The poem's first line establishes the situation as Snodgrass sees it: "There is no one here." That simple observation, as it grows more and more disquieting, compels the poem's two other concerns, one for the hard reality of the objects in the energized room, the other for the connection between this reality and the missing artist. But it is the artist's absence that first demands attention. The emptiness of the lower right quadrant of the painting seems both rigid in form and insubstantial. The artist cannot have gone anywhere, in the usual sense, but neither, in Snodgrass's view, has he held his ground. The room seems like quicksand. The artist's fate seems obvious: "His own room drank him."

This perception, which provides the pretext for the poem's development, should remind us that Snodgrass is not seeking traditional or even representative perspectives on the paintings that he chooses as his subjects. Other viewers might find in this painting not evidence of Matisse's "disappearance," but a strong sense of his controlling presence behind the canvas. That is, Matisse seems to be showing us his studio as he wants us to see it; he is instructing us in the appreciation of Matisse.

However, this more orthodox view depends on the viewer's also standing, as he is meant to, apart from the canvas. Snodgrass, to the contrary, must enter the painting to find, once he is inside its highly charged environment, that he is alone. Where is the artist? There can be but one explanation: he has sacrificed himself to his art.

The motive of the artist's self-sacrifice must be found, first, in the reality of the objects in the room, charged by the energized web of terra-cotta force in which they are suspended. All "environments of living" become energy—energy derived from the artist's destruction.

But how is this phenomenon to be understood? And how does the room, thriving on the energy released by the artist's sacrifice, communicate this energy to the depicted works of art? The dramatized viewer offers four corollaries, all approximate: the carnival ride in which bumper cars are powered through antennae tracing a charged ceiling; the ancient idea that the outermost, fiery empyrean sphere radiates its energy to earth; the theory suggesting ether as the basis of all matter and energy; and the medieval idea of God's love animating the universe. By a related process (we cannot know how closely related), the artist's creations obtain their reality and their energy from that given up by the artist.

"But," the poem concludes, "there is no one here." The near repetition of the opening line reminds us of the immense difference between simple observation and informed assertion. Having shared initially a bemused recognition of the artist's curious absence, we now share an understanding of that absence—tragic, profound, and grateful. The "matter" of the artist has been transformed into the "energy" of his works, just as the "matter" of the Matisse painting has itself been transformed into the "energy" of the imaginative response which is the poem.

III   "The Mother and Sister of the Artist"

After completing "The Red Studio," Snodgrass spent months searching for another painting he might use as the subject for a poem. Then, one day at Yaddo (a retreat for artists near Saratoga Springs, New York), the writer Josephine Herbst, looking through one of Snodgrass's books on the Post-Impressionists, came upon Edouard Vuillard's "Mother and Sister of the Artist." "Good Lord!" she cried. "Look at this horrid, tough old woman—and this

poor girl! She's simply being turned into wallpaper!" (*RP*, p. 71).
Miss Herbst thereby gave Snodgrass not only his next painting,
but also a response that could be developed in the poem. The tyran-
nical authority of the mother and frail vulnerability of the sister
were now obvious. Snodgrass's poem, then, would expose the
"terrifying domestic drama" lying beneath the surface of Vuillard's
world, traditionally regarded as one of discreet bourgeois charm.
Finding the terms in which to do so, however, proved no easy task.

Snodgrass found a helpful start in a remark by a young girl who
had once suffered from malnutrition. She looked at the mother in
the painting and remarked, "Well, she looks like *she* gets enough to
eat." Snodgrass's attention thus fell upon the dinner plate (on the
right edge of the canvas) and its importance in sustaining the structural line initiated by the faces of the mother and sister. "This apparent equation of plate and face must say something about the
devouring relationship between the woman and her daughter,"
Snodgrass decided (*RP*, p. 72). The essential difference between the
process portrayed in this painting and that represented by "The
Red Studio" became clear. While both are concerned with destruction, only one is concerned as well with creation. " 'The Red Studio'
had swallowed up its painter in order to give birth to his paintings,"
Snodgrass says. "Here, too, the girl was being swallowed alive by
the walls of a room but in order to give birth to nothing, or perhaps,
to undo the fact of her having got born at all" (*RP*, p. 73).

Then, having accumulated the substance of the poem, Snodgrass
chose as his dramatic premise one which he states in his subtitle;
because Vuillard would acquaint us with his mother and sister, with
the "mystery" of their "silent, modest" room,[6] Snodgrass will
provide "Instructions for the Visit." As we might expect, however,
given Snodgrass's dark reading of the painting, these instructions
are not ones that would facilitate our acquaintance. Their primary
intent is the dramatized visitor's self-preservation in a threatening
environment; they constitute a strategy for staying out of trouble.

The first step, we are told, is to pay proper compliments without
being intrusive. Observation of the proprieties enables us to proceed
with the visit.

Yet, as we approach more closely, the welcome we are to receive
is hardly encouraging:

> She will wait. And fix her steady
> Eyes on you—the straight stare
> Of an old politician.

Trying to say the right things will be little help; the old woman's stare will make short shrift of our courtesy. But if the strategy of a polite entrance is doomed, another must be sought.

The new strategy will be more direct, but its collapse, more sudden: "Try once to meet her eyes. But fail." Reference to the painting itself will substantiate the point. The eyes of both daughter and mother are rendered so roughly, as cavities in the impasto of the faces, that they do seem simultaneously vague and penetrating; they cannot be met.

The extent of the visitor's dilemma, our dilemma, is emphasized by the haste with which the direct strategy must be abandoned. The shift occupies only a single line in the "Instructions." Moreover, by recommending a protective pose of detachment and by listing strictures against any show of concern or curiosity, the new instructions realistically admit the impossibility of amicable introduction. They provide, at best, means toward an informed accommodation with the old woman's absolute control of her world, even as they provide subtle warnings against any attempt at intercession. Above all, they insist upon the visitor's keeping his nerve, maintaining his composure. The consequences of indiscretion, or even of obtaining too much knowledge of the situation, are uncertain but fearful.

That the instructions become admonitory at this point reveals the extent to which the fears aroused by the visit have overcome the interest that motivated it. We may imagine a ring of keys hanging by the mother's belt as a symbol of her repressive authority, but we must not seem to be looking for such a symbol. We may notice how the large household chest seems to rest on her back "like the monstrous pack / Of some enchanted pedlar," even as she seems to be "wrinkling / Like a potato" under it, but we must not ask why this chest, which both possesses and is possessed by her, "Has no knobs." We may begin to realize the awesome dimensions of her control over the household in general and this chest in particular, but we must not reveal our suspicion that the chest's contents "Could vanish at her / Will."

At this point in what is becoming more and more of an ordeal, we must be careful not only about the impression we make, but also about the awareness we obtain. Some thoughts must be avoided as resolutely as indiscretions. For instance, if the woman is in fact gaining in specific gravity, increasing in mass as she decreases in volume, her gravitational pull on her environment, already perceptible in the warped lines of perspective in the room, will become irresistible. Her authority will become a fatal vortex. She will be a "black hole" in her universe, and to the extent that we are a part of that universe, we may be drawn in and destroyed. But we cannot permit ourselves such fears, if we are to maintain our composure and thereby survive the visit.

As for the girl, we are advised to notice as little as possible, to avoid giving the impression that we can notice anything, and finally, to forget anything we have noticed. Her cuffs, "like cordovan restraints," her "half-fed, worrying eyes," her desperate self-effacement—these images of bondage and fear are oppressive enough. But what is truly terrifying is the growing awareness that, while we are observing someone being destroyed, we are powerless. The girl is already shapeless, "ethereal" in her dress, but we cannot intercede.

Once again, matter seems to be undergoing the transformation into energy. The old woman grows smaller and smaller as the girl fades away. But the increasing energy of the old woman can become only more voracious, and that released by the girl's dissolution is dissipated into the "empty twinkling" of air and wallpaper into which she fades.

That the poem ends with the visitor's observing an unforgettable scene he has been enjoined to forget reminds us just how paradoxical his position has been all along. His "instructions" place him in confrontation with an old woman who must not be (and cannot be) confronted, arouse in him fears that he must not hold, and direct his eyes to details that he "must not ever see." Insofar as he feels threatened by his situation, he is vulnerable; insofar as he feels even the slightest inclination to respond, he is impotent. This nightmarish paradox, the essence of the visitor's predicament, is also the basis of the poem's strength, its sustained subjective dichotomy.

The dramatic situation is far more vividly realized here than in "The Red Studio." There, the "visitor," a more objective observer, resolves a mystery. Here, the visitor finds himself implicated in the mystery, perhaps susceptible to its dark force. He must try to follow instructions that change frequently and may be contradictory at times. The unstated dangers that require particular defensive strategies are implied in the force of the poem's directives, just as the reality of one such danger, that of the old woman's "gravitational" attraction, is graphically conveyed by the diminution of the poem's lines as "the per- / spective drains / In her." Snodgrass's dramatic situation for "Vuillard: 'The Mother and

Sister of the Artist' " is effective not because it can accommodate the poet's ingenuity of association, as in "The Red Studio," but because it establishes and develops convincingly a sense of conflict, anxiety, and danger.

Yet, at the same time, the poem remains scrupulously faithful to its subject. Snodgrass's interpretation of the painting might well disturb the art critic, for it is not limited by the painting, but it is nevertheless inspired largely by features that are clearly observable. The sharply contrasting postures of the subjects; the use of a common palette for both the wall and the girl's dress; the matte, dimensionless black applied heavily to represent the mother's bulk (an earlier idea, a necklace, has been roughly obliterated on the mother's bodice)—these are the kinds of concrete details that sustain the poem's dramatic premise.

We have already noticed, for instance, how greatly a crucial turn in the poem depends on the way in which the mother's eyes have been painted. Vuillard represents the eyes of both the girl and her mother by laying down heavy splotches of the complexion ground in crude circular strokes; these strokes build up deep sockets that contain only the merest suggestions of eyes. Thus we cannot establish their focus, but the depth at which they are set against the high pallor of the faces gives an illusion of focus and penetration.

Or, as another example, while Snodgrass's sensitivity to Vuillard's manipulation of perspective may be somewhat exaggerated, the effect of the vortex at the painting's center is obvious to any viewer. The main subject of the painting represents a force capable of warping its environment, of bending to itself the lines of the floor, the window, and the chest. And the girl, subject to the centrifugal force generated at the edges of a strong centripetal one, dissolves into a wall become amorphous in order to receive her. The design of the wallpaper, executed with a deliberate neglect of foreshortening, defies principles of perspective just as surely as the lines of the room do.

Snodgrass has exercised a shaping imagination in writing the poem, to be sure, but he stays close to the painting at all times. The paradox of the visitor's simultaneous vulnerability and detachment arises here, for it is clearly part of Snodgrass's design that we confront Vuillard more directly by participating in the dilemmas that his art suggests. Thus, once again, the "matter" of a painting becomes the "energy" of response, and the poem which manifests that response both depends on and declares its independence of its subject.

IV   *"Les Nymphéas"*

The third of the poems on paintings articulates a response to one of the most celebrated paintings from Monet's "Les Nymphéas" series, the large, single canvas that occupies the entire western wall of one of the loveliest rooms at the Museum of Modern Art in New York City. In this case, Snodgrass's choice was deliberate. And, because the painting is not impressive in reproductions, it is clear that his choice resulted from an encounter with the painting itself; the response developed in the poem is one that depends on "sitting before it for long hours at the museum" (*RP*, p. 77).

It was this experience of contemplating the painting at length which convinced Snodgrass that he had discovered perhaps his best example so far of art transforming matter into energy. A sensation of personal vulnerability was again the means to this recognition. Snodgrass recalls his lengthy sessions with Monet: "I often had the sensation that if I did not get up and leave the room, the guards might well come in and find me missing" (*RP*, p. 77).

The obvious analogies are to his reading of "The Red Studio," in which he feels that the artist has sacrificed himself to give birth to his works, and that of "Mother and Sister of the Artist," in which he finds the girl being cast off and destroyed even as the visitor begins to fear the old woman's pull. But "Les Nymphéas" represents a different phenomenon; though it might want to absorb a visitor intent on absorbing it, it would do so out of love. "It so obviously wanted me," Snodgrass says, "so truly loved me" (*RP*, p. 77).

The means by which the painting exerts this attraction are not difficult to discern. Its initial appeal is its color, a palette rich in subtly variegated pastels. However, when the chatoyant masses begin to resolve into recognizable forms, the effect of the work becomes more complex and pronounced. As Snodgrass has described this process in his essay (*RP*, p. 76), we perceive the pond in three stages. First we see, through the mist, the water's surface with the lilies floating on it; then we discern the clouds, which are overhead, as they seem to float *beneath* the lilies; finally we see, or seem to, the plants on the bottom.

The painting thus provides, as Snodgrass says, "a very strange perspective on the world" (*RP*, p. 76). But this strange perspective is at the same time precisely realistic. Monet painted what he saw. But what he saw was the lily pond he had built to express his conception of nature as "mysterious, infinite, and unpredictable."[7] In it he found a world, as William Seitz has said, "new to art, ultimately spherical in its allusions, within which the opposites of above and below, close and distant, transparent and opaque, occupied and empty are conflated."[8]

There is much in the painting, then, that can free the viewer from a secure balance within the familiar dimensions of the world. By abolishing the usual frames of spatial reference, the painting can effect in the viewer a liberating vertigo, a sense of being drawn, as Snodgrass says, "into the center of the picture, into the vortex of these gray waters" (RP, pp. 76 - 77).

But to what end? To substantiate his feeling that the painting's intent is to compel surrender to sensation, Snodgrass concentrated on Monet's celebrated devotion to light—his insistence on depicting not objects themselves but, rather, the light that objects emanate at a particular time of day under particular conditions. For Snodgrass, the effect of this fidelity to light is not only that Monet's paintings record the energy of light rather than the matter of objects, but also that they suggest the dissolution of the objects' reality in favor of the greater reality of the energy they reflect. Working on this assumption and on the sensation of imminent dissolution given the faithful viewer, Snodgrass finds the painting one intended "to break down the armoring of the self and its beliefs and ideas, so that one might become an energy among energies, open to the flux of experience, absorbing and being absorbed by sensation" (RP, p. 79).

In the poems on "The Red Studio" and "Mother and Sister of the Artist," Snodgrass had to devise dramatic situations capable of coherently uniting the diverse associations and ideas he had already accumulated. But for "Les Nymphéas" he found the dramatic situation first. It lay in his own sense of willing engulfment in the painting's seductive depths, his own desire to join the "radiance" that might be found there. The speaker in this poem is not a guide, but a participant in the painting.

The poet offers no solutions, for no problems are to be solved. He uses no imperatives, for he has no instructions to give. The speaker's concern is not so much our understanding or propriety of conduct as his own experience. And because this experience involves the surrender of "beliefs and ideas" in favor of energy, flux, and sensation, its chronicle can hardly take the form of logical exposition. In the world of "Les Nymphéas," logic no longer serves, but rapture awaits those willing to shed "the armoring of the self." As the speaker passes from the early glimpses of recognition to the warm fluorescence of energy in flux, only the language of rapture—rhapsodic, free, ambiguous—will serve.

However, the trance-like quality of the poem's language need not deter us from attempting to describe the effects it produces and how it produces them. Snodgrass may be attempting to represent an experience of abandonment, but he never relinquishes control of the poem. Even as the poem's ambiguities and abstractions may frustrate our attempts to reduce it to literal statement, we can recognize the significance of such frustration and develop a reading that respects it.

Such a reading must begin with the poem's first three lines, which establish the particular form of consciousness that is to prevail throughout: it is the semiconsciousness of the moment between sleep and waking, when the awareness of light first intrudes. It is this consciousness that accepts the suggestive, dislocated universe discovered in the lines that follow; it is this consciousness that penetrates its own perceptions to obtain visions that encompass all of time, all of sensation.

The opening psalmic hymn of Creation (which reflects sound historical geology, curiously) expresses an initial awareness of the painting; the response is to the effect of the whole, to the "downdrifting" that occupies the entire canvas. In the terms of the painting, the mist, the waters, the algae are universal; the pond embodies all creation, for it is capable of receiving and reflecting light, which is infinite.

Having sensed the eternal cycle of rising and falling, the eternal flux of matter and energy, the speaker now begins to see emerging from the mists vague and lovely forms, neither rising nor falling, but "passing."

The bobbing passage of island-like mists and mist-like islands, reminiscent of the eerie glow of the *ignis fatuus* (swamp-fire), of the rose-purple flowers of swamp milkweed, and of the warmth of lanterns borne through a still but heavy snowfall, provides a model for the speaker's own experience. The horizontal flux in the context of the vertical one suggests that accommodation of time to eternity which he has sensed, though fragmentarily, in "the memory of women." Such memory receives us, "bobbing" and "blinking," and would seem to arrest and preserve us, but it, too, is part of the flux; it participates in eternity yet is constantly "passing."

The speaker's visions and intuitions have by this point begun to

arouse in him the awareness that to enter the flux, to become "an
energy among energies," requires his surrender, "a yielding up of
the self." And while he has already obtained glimpses of the rapture
to be found through such surrender, he can still recognize its
frightening uncertainty:

> Within those depths
> What ravening? What devouring rage?
> How shall our living know its ends of yielding?

The implied answer, clearly, is that the full consciousness of the intact self cannot know what dangers lie in the depths of submission
to sensation; it cannot know, at least not in advance, what will be
the consequences of surrender, the "ends of yielding."

All that can be understood of such submission must come through
sensation itself. Rational analogies are of little help. The speaker
describing the process must rely on an objective correlative:

> These things have taken me as the mouth an orange—
> That acrid sweet juice entering every cell;
> And I am shared out.

Having opened the armor of his self to the sensations he has experienced, having surrendered his "matter" to the energy of the
painting, the speaker can now absorb and be absorbed. He can
become the "water lilies . . . mayflies . . . whirled dust" of a world
continually uniting the primeval and existential. He can become
"an energy among energies," part of the "Fluorescence into which
we pass and penetrate." And he can do so joyfully, lovingly; the
painting wants him: "O soft as the thighs of women; / O radiance,
into which I go on dying . . ."

There is no full stop because there can be none. The process of
surrender is continual, and it leads the speaker not to a conclusion
but into a potential. He will "go on dying" into the radiance, surrendering himself to and becoming energy.

In the "Preface" to *In Radical Pursuit*, Snodgrass cites the
familiar post-Freudian assumption that man is to a considerable
degree the creature of the "darker, less visible areas of emotion and
personality" (p. xii). And many of his poems do develop the bleaker
implications of this assumption. Yet man's capacity for recognizing
and responding to the subliminal forces that propel him can be
beneficial as well. Hence, we need not regard "Les Nymphéas" as a

flight from reality; it represents a concession to a truer reality that can be found in the energy throbbing beneath the surface of paint and canvas. As in the first two of Snodgrass's poems on paintings, the matter of the art work is transformed into the energy of response. But here, for the first time, the matter of the speaker's self is transformed into the energy of the painting. The poem absorbs the painting; the painting absorbs the poem.

V   *"The Execution of the Emperor Maximilian"*

Snodgrass's affinity for paintings that represent processes of destruction and dissolution would seem to make his next choice, "The Execution of the Emperor Maximilian," by Edouard Manet, an obvious one. Its subject is an historical event that, to its contemporaries, represented not only the destruction of a ruler, but a grim portent for the empire he represented. To contemporary viewers, the painting's detached and austere handling of its subject seemed a deliberate exacerbation of their anxieties and sense of loss; as Snodgrass's analysis of the painting suggests, Manet's painting may have seemed more portentous than the earlier news of the event itself.

Snodgrass certainly finds broad historical implications in the painting. Its emphasis on the firing squad rather than the condemned man, together with its refusal to identify Maximilian, signifies for him the full extent of the emperor's loss of authority.[9] In the painting's "uncentered lighting and the apparent diversity of shadows," Snodgrass finds implicit "the rise of individualism, of democracy, of relativism" (*RP*, p. 83), consequences of the breakdown in authoritarian government. In the arbitrary perspective made obvious in the wall's cutting off the parade ground from the countryside, Snodgrass reads a message of futility; action beyond the most immediate range is without effect. The implied insignificance of the emperor's death can thus be seen as an expression of "the breakdown of philosophical matter, the loss of religious centrality" (*RP*, p. 83). Finally, the painting's implied reference to a crucifixion scene, which Snodgrass thinks parodic, may suggest not only the "decay and death of Christianity," but of all religion (*RP*, p. 84).

That the painting can in fact sustain such a heavy burden of inference may seem doubtful, but Snodgrass does ground his sense of the work's portentousness on specific details within it. More importantly, he derives thereby the perspective that enables him to find in the Manet painting the same kinds of forces he discovered in the Matisse and Vuillard. Imagination takes precedence, as it should, over critical constraints.

Yet the Manet is different in important ways from the other paintings. In solving the mystery of Matisse's empty studio, in revealing the insidious malice of Vuillard's mother, or in probing the enchanting depths of Monet's lily pond, Snodgrass has been able to assume the artist's engagement with his subject. But Manet's painting, though it depicts a particular historical moment, suggests no such engagement. Manet depicts the execution with, as Georges Bataille has said, "the same indifference as if he had chosen a fish or flower for his subject."[10] He is not merely objective, noncommittal; he depicts an event that had horrified all of Europe as though it were only "a firing exercise." Instead of developing the dramatic content of an empty studio, a domestic scene, or a lily pond, Manet ignores that of a notorious execution.

If the painting were our only source of information on the execution, we would have to conclude that "neither the soldiers nor the Emperor and his companions were conscious of the reasons which had brought them together at that particular moment."[11] Manet seems entirely unwilling to interpret the scene for his viewers; he "puts the facts before them but disdainfully refuses to confide to them the emotion that he feels."[12] Indeed, Manet seems to have converted the hot energy of public reaction into the cool matter of paint and canvas, thereby reversing the process Snodgrass discerns in the other paintings.

The "obvious" choice was, then, not so obvious. Manet chooses a subject that should be dramatic, but he achieves in "The Execution of the Emperor Maximilian" a remarkable degree of emotional reticence. An attempt to uncover a latent energy of implicit drama would thus do violence to the painting's deliberately nondramatic rendering and to Manet's manifest indifference. So, in order to discover a feasible dramatic situation, Snodgrass had to look beyond the painting itself.

Doing so, he perceived that a clear paradox—the angry public reaction aroused by an emotionally neutral painting—was itself dramatic. Manet's indifference to his subject and to the response his painting would provoke provoked a vehement public response; the dearth of emotion in the painting stirred emotions. The cool matter of the painting thus became the fuel for energetic reaction: a dramatic situation. All that remained for Snodgrass was to find some means of compelling us to participate, to experience Manet's painting with the eyes and hearts of Manet's contemporaries.

Snodgrass begins by developing incompatible voices. The voice that constitutes the main strand of the poem represents "much what a puzzled viewer might say to himself on seeing the picture for the first time" (*RP*, p. 84). The language is "prosy, matter-of-fact," just like the painting. The other voice, Snodgrass says, is heard in "sections of highly poetical prose . . . meant to sound like snippets from partisan newspapers, biographies, or histories" (*RP*, p. 84). In the conflict of these two voices would lie some echo of the contemporary clash between the painting and public attitude.

The only difficulty with this description is that the voices cannot be so easily characterized. Snodgrass's distinction between two voices in the poem is helpful, but it cannot be uncritically applied, for neither voice becomes a caricature of itself; neither is static.

Indeed, one of the poem's signal achievements is that it conveys a sense of discord between opposing voices without providing a sure sense of balance between them. Suspended between judgment and emotion, detachment and engagement, the reader's dilemma is analogous to that of Manet's contemporaries. He can share their sense of impending dissolution as well as their need to resist it.

The situation begins to develop with the opening "snippet," which accomplishes two purposes: it places us in the dramatic action of the event and suggests the futile courage of the main actor. He is a willing victim: "Aim well, muchachos; aim right / here," he points to his heart. A man at the point of death is behaving well, we learn through an apparent eyewitness report.

But the alternate voice that follows echoes in an art gallery. It is that of Snodgrass's viewer, "puzzled" before Manet's painting, attentive to its details but unsure as to their significance. The delicate postures taken by the firing squad, their colorful European uniforms, and their almost sportive absorption in their task are curious but do not seem tragic. It is almost as though each is lining up a shot in billiards. The one soldier who stands with his back to the scene, looking "less like a penguin" than the rest, may have "turned up late." Or he may be an officer, preparing his rifle to administer the *coup de grâce*. He *may* be. But, as the viewer says, "Who knows?"

The second and third short passages reassert the narrative and descriptive points of view. The first of these, a report on the moment of death, emphasizes a pathetic detail, the necessity of a second volley for Maximilian. He had asked to be "shot in the body so that his / mother might see his face." But the passage is more matter-of-fact than "high-flown." It asserts no emotional response, though one should be produced by the information it conveys. The other passage reveals somewhat less restraint. Its style is still not particularly "high-flown," but its choice of details suggests a more tragic view of Maximilian's death. The subtle combination of the historical and the metaphysical—the state funeral for Maximilian's body and the chapel for his soul—asserts the significance of Maximilian's death and assumes its meaning in a world supported by the divine order.

Just this sense of order and meaning is missing in Manet's depiction of the event, though, as the increasingly sophisticated remarks of the viewer make clear. In the second and third primary sections, the viewer concentrates on those details in the painting that suggest the insignificance of the execution.

For instance, the peasant spectators, attracted by a show of pageantry, appear bored and uncomprehending. Their detachment from what they are seeing corresponds precisely to their own insignificance, implicit in the cursory technique (expertly) employed to render their heads. They seem no more sensitive than the rocks of the wall on which they lean.

"Surely someone must come / Declare significance," muses the viewer, as in behalf of those behind the wall. His questions must be much the same as theirs. But the painting to him, like the event to the spectators, remains mute.

To this point in the poem, the most obvious contrasts between its voices involve not so much their styles as their assumptions and expectations. The primary voice, that of the "puzzled" viewer observing the painting for the first time, is attentive, objective, and skeptical. But its supposed "matter-of-factness" is qualified considerably by speculation ("Who / Will ever know?"), irony ("Surely someone must come. . ."), analogy (". . . like some child's two-penny crucifixion"), and imagery ("An inkling of quiet streams, or pine-shadowed lanes"). Indeed, the spare verse of the first three "snippets" seems the more "matter-of-fact," the less "high-flown," though its effectiveness in inviting an emotional response is more clear.

There are more important differences. While the first voice represents a response to a work of art, the second represents descriptions of and exposition about an event. While the first is controlled, at least at first, by the attitude of cool detachment that the painting expresses, the other reflects contemporary concern with practical consequences. So the primary result of the competition between the two voices to this point is a sense of the substantial difference between the interests of an historian (whether "partisan" or not) and those of the painterly artist, Manet.

Even these distinctions between the voices become somewhat less clear in the conclusion, however. The final three short passages offer an ironic historical footnote, an unemotional summary of Maximilian's curious "success," and a brief biographical chronology. Although all three give us more information about (and thus more sympathy for) the emperor, none is a frank appeal for emotional response. Even the style of the second "snippet," which speaks of Maximilian's "true vocation; as / martyr and sacrificial victim," seems "matter-of-fact." The short passages do express a perspective from which the execution of Maximilian is significant and consequential, but this perspective, though alien to Manet's painting, seldom seems to reveal "high-flown emotional interpretations."

The most highly "poetical" lines in the poem, in fact, are those of the primary voice in its final two sections. By providing additional information about Maximilian, these sections make him more touching, even as they clarify the nature of the "puzzled" viewer's puzzlement.

Presumably "seeing the picture for the first time," the dramatized viewer is extraordinarily well-informed about Maximilian's fantastical political, religious, and humanitarian ambitions, knows of the aftermath of his death, and can imagine his fondest hopes. Yet even more revealing than his knowledge of Maximilian is his attempt to say something for him. He makes such an attempt four times in the final section, grasping at all he knows of the man, until he must concede the ultimate frustration provided by Manet's painting: not only does it fail to emphasize the emperor, it fails even to identify him.

"Which IS the man?" That is the question, and no attention to dress ("who gets shot in a frock coat and sombrero?"), expression ("In that man's bland face we see nothing, not that firm / Nobility which we demand. . ."), or situation ("Perhaps it's this one, standing there / Spread-legged. . .") will provide an answer. The only answer available is that one of the victims, "whoever he was, is all finished being." Maximilian, who either is this man or shares his fate, becomes at once irrelevant, and no mere chronology of his life, such as that in the final "snippet," can certify the reality of his existence. With the conclusive frustration of the viewer's attempt to find some meaning to Maximilian's death through Manet's painting, the drama of the poem ends.

But it has proved high drama, as one tentative judgment after another has failed to acquit itself as credible or pertinent. None, finally, proves "correct." And, to the extent that we can participate in the dramatic but futile efforts of the viewer to discover meaning, we share the energy of his growing despair. Matter has again become energy, but only because Manet succeeds so thoroughly in denying the energy of an event through the matter of his canvas and paints.

One final question remains: How are we to reconcile Snodgrass's descriptions of his opposing voices with our experience of the poem? His direct distinction between matter-of-factness and high-flown emotion seems to do little justice to the subtlety of the contrasts that develop. But his distinction does suggest the polarities against which the voices move; Snodgrass establishes a standard enabling us to see more clearly the variations that he works.

VI *"The Starry Night"*

Van Gogh's "The Starry Night" was the first slide chosen by Snodgrass's two students during his single class session of modern art appreciation, and it was his first thought when the art magazine solicited a poem. But he decided a poem on "The Starry Night" would require more time than he had been given because its style would be one he had deliberately avoided in his poetry. "I had spent years unlearning such stylistic violence," Snodgrass says (*RP*, p. 65).

But the problem of style Snodgrass faced when he finally did approach the Van Gogh led him to concentrate on its structural balances and juxtapositions, especially those relating the still church at the poem's center and the bright, violent, disorderly sky. There he found again the leitmotiv of his series of poems, "the theme of matter and energy." His only remaining problem was that of developing an appropriate form for his ideas.

By Snodgrass's own account, the construction of this poem, stage by stage, proved particularly methodical. He began by choosing alternating styles, as in the Manet poem. The "split between order and disorder" that organizes the painting would organize the poem as well. And when the result of such alternation began to seem "too 'regular', too easy," Snodgrass decided to "scattershot" quotations from Van Gogh's letters. And when even the result of this combination of elements began to seem "too arbitrary, conscious, and contrived," Snodgrass decided on one further element, a series of variations on a "set of sounds" found in Van Gogh's last words (*RP*, pp. 90 - 91).

A poem that combines contrasting voices, "scattershot" quotations, and subtle, cumulative variations on a set of sounds imposes a formidable responsibility on its readers. Obviously, as we read the poem, we must be alert throughout for the effects of juxtaposed voices, of interruptive quotations, and of verbal echoes. Yet at the same time, if we are to read critically, we must be attentive to the development of each element. There are also two larger questions: Is the poem as a whole greater than the sum of its parts? Does it, for all its complexity and difficulty, convey to us the energy so abundant in the matter of Van Gogh's masterpiece?

The poem begins with a neutral but unconventional stanza (perhaps both "simple" and "scattered"?) that establishes a dynamic relationship between the painting's subjects. The frequent, arbitrary caesurae emphasize the contrast between town ("Only the little / town . . . only this little / still") and sky ("all shock and dazzle"). But the prosodic breaks also have the effect of simulating the breathless attention inspired by an initial encounter with the painting. Sky and town can be studied, more or less carefully, later on, but one's first inclination is to exclaim, with Snodgrass's student, "There's not one thing in that whole painting that will stand still except that little church, there, at the center!" (*RP*, p. 64).

The town, as Snodgrass describes it in his "simple" style, is a citadel of order and interdependency. "Row on row . . . Edge over edge . . . Face by face . . . Plane over plane . . . ," the cottages, cottage roofs, stones, and walls of the town stand in a timeless pattern "old as a memory." And the "still dead-center" of this pattern, toward which the slate roofs ascend, is the village chapel, "tiny as a child's toy / And as far." In one sense, as the two interspersed quotations remind us, the chapel had been "a child's toy," for it is that served by Van Gogh's clergyman father during his childhood. But this chapel, the "hurricane's eye" of the painting's tumultuous universe, is also the only part of the town that dares "the sky's rush." Its dark spire, upheld by the salients of the church and the "stone stairs" of the town's converging roofs, is "keen as

your mother's needle / Pricking the horizon." Still and dark, the
chapel may seem a lighthouse "where there shines / No light," but
its firmness provides the town (and thus the painting and the poem)
with a bridge from town to sky.

After the steady, well-organized description of the town (in which
we hear another kind of balance, between sibilants and quan-
titatively long vowels, e.g., "keen as your mother's needle / Pricking the horizon"), a single word announces a startling shift of style
and subject:

> Overhead: suns; stars; blind
> tracers bursting; pustules;
> swamp mouths of old violence. . . .

This eruptive catalog, "wilder" in style than the description of the
town, gives an impression, as does Van Gogh's sky, of being
"scattered and slapdash." But, like Van Gogh's sky, in which each
brushmark is a calculated means to an intended impression, the
passage also reveals a conscious design.

The frantic listing of uncontainable and indescribable phenomena, with its intimations of tumult and anarchy, resolves finally into
a rich image of creation reminiscent of that in "Les Nymphéas."
Van Gogh's sky may suggest the "fusing / destroying / burning"
essential to the transformation of chaos into the created universe,
but, at the same time, it reminds us that the art and energy of creation are continually manifest in the "trails of vapor" that span every
starry night, tumbling like (we should be alert to the sound of the
phrase) "the high / gods on Garganos."

Van Gogh's acute commentary on Giotto and Cimabue, thir-
teenth-century artists and architects, provides an appropriate signal
for the poem's return to town. (If Snodgrass indeed "scattershot"
the Van Gogh quotations, he has enjoyed splendid good fortune!)
The quality Van Gogh sees in the monolithic solidity of thirteenth-
century Italian society is precisely that attributed to Van Gogh's
town by Snodgrass's first "town" sequence.

The development of this idea occupies the second "town" sequence, which begins by marshaling observations on the town's
quiet structural order, then considers the lives that must be lived
amid such order. Walls protect, but they also contain. Those leading
"ordered lives" within these walls and under a magnificent and
threatening sky seem "Like climbers huddled to a rock ledge,

pigs / Snuffling their trough, rooting at their dam." The compact efficient structure of the town provides a calm below the cosmic storm, but it is the chill, static calm of Keats' Grecian urn:

> Down those dark lanes you cannot see
> A lantern moving or a shadow sway,
> No dog howls, and your ear will never know
> The footfall of some prowler, some lover's tread,
> Some wandered, long gone,
>   . . . who cannot return.

This second examination of the town, deeper and more conjectural than the first, is punctuated by three fragments that provide a subtle, distant counterpoint. The main passage moves from observations on the town's order, through assumptions regarding the ordered lives within, to a recognition of the suspension in which town and people are caught up; they rest in the perfection of their security. Simultaneously, the fragments suggest a contrary motion: an image of the community (*"Every individual a stone and / the stones clung together"*) leads to an oblique, more narrow, reference to a personal dilemma of some kind. And the next reference is even more specific, to *"four great crises"* of self-knowledge, *"when I did not know what / I said, what I wanted, even what I did."*

Van Gogh's stricture against *"revolutionaries"* with *"hollow dreams"* effectively marks the next shift in the poem, from the staid, inanimate town of "ordered lives" to the furious, voracious mountains that lie behind and threaten to approach it, "murderous as the seasons, / bluer than the years." But the shift is more than topographical, for the description of the mountains, "shuddering" in their lust for the town, is repeatedly interrupted by outbursts of mountainous passion from Van Gogh's letters. The transitional fragment suggests a distinction between instincts, which are easily satisfied, and passions, which can bring pain.

This distinction is implicit throughout. The mountains threaten to overwhelm the town in a tidal wave of broken stone, and the town's order and security already seem all too vulnerable to "its feathery surf." The "groves of olives" become "gardens / of agony," this time because of suffering they themselves endure. The easy, ordered satisfaction of the instincts, domesticated by society for the public good, sustains the little town. But the threat hangs over its head.

Van Gogh, though unable or unwilling to settle for the sober complacency of satisfied instincts—

> *Painting*
> *and much screwing are not*
> *compatible; man . . .*
> *becomes ambitious as soon as he*
> *becomes impotent.*

—has felt the "waves" and has learned their passion: "*I feel a storm of / desire to embrace something. . . .*"
The obvious response would be that Van Gogh embraces his art, that a painting like "The Starry Night" is the fruit of his passions. But Snodgrass's poem also shows Van Gogh as his letters reveal him, a man struck by desire, even in the act of denying it, for "*a woman, a sort / of domestic hen.*" Set into the description of the hungry, shuddering mountains, Van Gogh's words suggest the deprivation suffered by one "long gone . . . who cannot return."
Yet, those who have stayed, as another transitional quotation from Van Gogh's letters suggests, may be victims of a far worse fate:

> *In spring, a caged bird feels strongly*
> *there is something he should be doing.*
> *But what was it? He gets vague ideas.*
> *The children say, but he has everything*
> *he wants.*

The final sustained description of the town is the most penetrating and conjectural. The few lights in the town, on streets hidden from view, inspire a viewer's imagination, but provide him with little factual illumination. The town is preserved from the sky by its security on the canvas; it is fixed and still. We may think what we wish,

> But nothing moves
> In those dark streets which you can never see,
> No one is walking or will ever walk there
> Now, and you will never know. . . .

All that now remains to be considered is the large, flame-shaped cypress that dominates the entire lower left quadrant of the painting. Fierce and vital, it "mocks / the thin blue spire" of the church.

Like that before the gates of Eden, this sword bars our way and enforces our distance from the town, even as it has driven us (and Van Gogh) out.

Yet, from the distance enforced by the painting, the town seems to emerge all the more clearly as a haven protecting the kinds of domesticity glanced at in the interruptive quotations from the letters. The town is lifeless, but it lies "peacefully" in "Some middle distance of the past," secure on a canvas maintaining its "*calm even in the catastrophe.*" The "Fierce heaven" lies overhead, but it is accessible in only one way: "*We take death to reach a star. . . .*" And meanwhile, as the last words of the passionate, suffering artist seem to take shape even before they are spoken, the town rests

> And still so calm
> and still
> so still

The last words of the poem are Van Gogh's last. In his native Flemish, they mean, Snodgrass tells us in a note, "This is the way to go," "I'd like to die like this," or "I want to go home." But if we have been attentive to persistent affinities of sound (such as those in the quotations immediately above), we will discover in the Flemish itself a prepared sense of inevitability. Not only are the sounds of the phrase insistently familiar, but they can be heard as the soft, final notes in a careful diminuendo sustained through the last twenty lines of the poem. After all the tumult of sky, mountains, and cypress, there remains the peace of the little town, which its wanderer, "long gone," found only with his last words, "*Zóó heen kan gaan.*"

CHAPTER 7

The Führer Bunker

PUBLISHED as a "work in progress" in June 1977, *The Führer Bunker* promises to become as controversial and influential as *Heart's Needle* proved to be. Its subject, the personalities and events involved in Hitler's final days, is itself fascinating and still highly provocative. More important, by means of the soliloquy and dramatic monologue, Snodgrass has given the notorious speakers in his poems an immediate dramatic presence that histories of the period do not and cannot provide. Working from both a poet's imagination and an historian's commitment to truth, Snodgrass has the principal figures of the Third Reich reveal themselves by speaking in our presence. We are allowed to overhear them. And what we hear are things the speakers "never would have said to anyone, perhaps not even to themselves" (II, p. 401).[1]

Moreover, the most crucial issues in the poem, freedom of the will and the nature of betrayal, are as vital to contemporary observers as to historians of World War II—perhaps more so. *The Führer Bunker* raises questions that failed to die in the ashes of Hitler's final refuge. They remain vexing problems in these poems because, for the most part, Snodgrass ignores conventional judgments and avoids making explicit moral judgments himself. The reader, subjected to different voices and interpretations of events, must remain on guard, make his own judgments, and be willing to revise them. For the poems, as Snodgrass admits, "do leave you free to choose the Nazis" (I, p. 308).

The poetic forms through which we hear the voices of Speer, Hitler, Goebbels, and the like are as diverse as the characters they reveal. In the "Heart's Needle" cycle, there is a similar variety of forms, but here the various forms are even more closely related to particular speakers and their situations. "Each speaker has a kind of verse form that is typical of his or her personality," Snodgrass points out, and they range from the "waspish couplets" of Goebbels to the fancy French forms through which his wife speaks (I, p. 304). As is the case with "Heart's Needle," the reasons for such formal diversity go beyond the requirements of simple dramatic decorum. Once again, the poet seeks to exploit the subliminal effects of the sound of his poems, to produce poetry so rich "that the meaning lies at very deep levels" (II, p. 405).

In short, the subject of *The Führer Bunker* startles us, its moral relativism challenges us, and its stylistic virtuosity alerts us to its richness and complexity. Like "Heart's Needle," *The Führer Bunker* is a bold enterprise rising unexpectedly from the mainstream. When asked how his new poems fit the context of contemporary American poetry, Snodgrass replied, "My hope is that they don't" (I, p. 307).

I *Approaching the Bunker*

Like many ambitious works of art, *The Führer Bunker* is both an artistic "event" and a literary "achievement." To understand the event, we must appreciate the interests, literary models, and experiences that have influenced and encouraged its conception. To understand the achievement, we must be able to discern within the poem its inner history: the extent to which the poem reflects and builds upon what the poet has done before, and the extent to which it represents a new direction for him. Neither approach is any substitute, of course, for sensitive reading of the poem itself, but both can provide helpful approaches.

The deepest roots of *The Führer Bunker* strike all the way to the final days of Hitler and the personalities attached to him. Snodgrass's interest in the Nazi period began as soon as the war was over. Soon after his discharge from the Pacific Fleet, he began reading all that he could find about the Nazi period, for he found the emerging record of horrific acts and mean ambitions both fascinating and beyond immediate comprehension. "I really wanted to know what the hell could somebody think, or feel, that would make them feel those acts were necessary. How could they even think they were possible?" (I, p. 298).

One 1947 study, H. R. Trevor-Roper's *The Last Days of Hitler*, was an early influence and has proved a continuing one. This study of the personalities and events of the final weeks of Hitler's life, written by a British historian and intelligence officer charged with the responsibility for the record, is all the more dramatic for its sober reliance on available facts. Within a year or two of the book's publication, Snodgrass began trying to write a play based on the Trevor-Roper material. "That didn't work," he recalls. "I had rather poor teachers, and I wasn't very good" (I, p. 298).

Snodgrass abandoned the play, but not his interest in questions raised by the behavior of the Third Reich's leaders and hangers-on. He went on, as we have seen, to write poems that seem far removed from his specific interest in World War II. Yet his experimentation with different forms, his attempts at multivoiced poems (e.g., "Van Gogh: 'The Starry Night' "), and his continuing concerns with issues of responsibility and fidelity were to provide a means by which his dormant fascination with the Hitler material might one day achieve poetic expression.

Then, in the early 1970s, Snodgrass began to experiment with his ideas of history, using the soliloquy and dramatic monologue. Several of Browning's dramatic monologues, such as "Mr. Sludge, 'The Medium' " and "Bishop Blougram's Apology," were important to him, he recalls. But of particular importance was a long cycle of poems about espionage and betrayal, *The War of the Secret Agents* by Henri Coulette (1966). Snodgrass admired the book at once. "The first thing I felt . . . before I ever analyzed it at all, was, yes, that feels right, that's the way the world feels" (I, p. 301). He found the different voices in the cycle's seventeen poems authentic and exciting and its dramatic premise equally so. "You have a World War II situation, in which a whole bunch of British secret agents were sent to France and all caught by the Germans and killed. The British betrayed them. They were sent there to be caught, so that real secret agents wouldn't be noticed" (I, p. 299). Only later did Snodgrass learn, to his horror, that the poem is based on fact. It seems reasonable to surmise that his admiration for this book, together with his surprised recognition of its factual basis, may have enabled him to glimpse once again the artistic possibilities of his own historical concerns.

The most immediate impetus for *The Führer Bunker* may have come, however, from two experiences Snodgrass had while participating in panel discussions. As a member of one panel, he found himself with Allen Ginsberg and LeRoi Jones (now Imamu Amiri Baraka). Snodgrass recalls the experience vividly: "They were calling me every filthy name and talking about what a rotten fascist I was and how dreadful and horrible" (I, p. 299). When the moderator attempted to restore order by asking the panel to articulate what they thought wrong with American civilization, Jones pointed to Snodgrass and said, "He's what's wrong with American civilization." Snodgrass's reaction? "What a compliment!" "I started thinking about that and decided: if only it were true! If one could identify with *all* that evil, he ought to be one hell of a poet. And I suppose the *Bunker* is one way to try that" (II, p. 407).

As a member of a similar panel, he joined Ralph Ellison and a few others in a discussion of the dramatic hero. Ellison objected to Snodgrass's broad definition of the concept by pointing out that it would enable one to write "tragedy" about the notorious and the despicable. "It means you or I could write a *tragedy* about Madam Nhu," he said, referrring to the powerful representative of South Vietnam's repressive Diem government in the early 1960s. "That's just horrifying," Ellison concluded. A few minutes later, after the conversation had turned to other subjects, Ellison changed his mind. "That's right!" Snodgrass remembers his saying. "If I had been there—a Catholic lady, raised in that situation, with a chance for power—I might well have become like that. I *could* do what she did" (II, p. 407). Ellison's turnabout prodded Snodgrass to reconsider the possibility of a tragedy of evil, and when his interest in Madam Nhu was frustrated by a lack of sufficient information, he turned again to Hitler.

Recalling both panels, Snodgrass concludes, "I am sure that being willing to identify with what you think is evil is perhaps what is most crucial to the making of a work of art that has some kind of breadth" (II, pp. 407 - 408).

Such are the circumstances that bear on the artistic "event." To approach the "achievement" of the poem, however, we must observe the extent to which it represents coherent growth, the fruition of sustained artistic concerns. Only if we appreciate how closely related *The Führer Bunker* is in important ways to Snodgrass's earlier poetry can we begin to evaluate his fresh initiatives in the poem.

First, *The Führer Bunker* continues a gradual progression in Snodgrass's work toward a much more objective subject matter. As we have seen, his most important early poems are highly personal ones, so intimate and candid as to seem "confessional." In *After Experience*, there appears to be an attempt to develop a more objective view of personal experience. The collection is notable also for subjects further and further removed from the domestic experience of the poet. Snodgrass often considers his own presence in the world, but his concern with the world itself grows steadily deeper. In *The Führer Bunker*, Snodgrass finally chooses a subject that he knows about only through secondary sources and through discussions with a few persons who had a personal involvement. From poems that were clearly "in the poet," Snodgrass has moved to write poems thoroughly "in the world."

Second, *The Führer Bunker* sustains Snodgrass's continuing concern as an artist with being "as relativistic as possible." Though Snodgrass's relativism is crucial to these poems about monstrous human beings, it is not an attitude adopted for temporary artistic ends. Snodgrass's distrust of moral absolutes permeates his entire work. It informs the struggle for understanding in "Heart's Needle" and lies at the heart of such poems as "A Visitation."

But relativism is of particular importance to *The Führer Bunker*, where Snodgrass pursues his announced aim "to stretch the reader's psyche" by "aggression against the reader's narrow definitions of himself and what he believes and what he thinks" (I, p. 303). The reader who would be capable of seeing and knowing more of the world must first surrender his sense of moral superiority, distrust his conventional beliefs about right and wrong, and recognize the evil of which he might be capable. Among other things, *The Führer Bunker* is an attempt to push the reader in this direction.

Third, *The Führer Bunker* extends the treatment of one of the most prominent themes in all of Snodgrass's work, the importance of personal autonomy and the related necessity for assertion of the will. "We try to choose our life," the dramatized poet of "Heart's Needle" tells his daughter. Man must first wish "to be, to act, to live," Spinoza says in "After Experience Taught Me. . . ." *The Führer Bunker*, however, dramatizes two examples of the corruption of this principle. Through the course of the cycle, Hitler indulges himself in the delusion of total autonomy. Yet he is unable in any way at all to "choose his life." As Snodgrass says, Hitler "sees himself as acting in a way completely free," but he is, in fact, "absolutely and completely *un*free, because he is at the mercy of some dreadful inner compulsion which he has no recognition of—or very little" (I, p. 297).

Speer, on the other hand, is a man who has voluntarily sacrificed his autonomy. As Trevor-Roper says, "Supposing politics to be irrelevant, he turned aside, and built roads and bridges and factories, while the logical consequences of government by madmen emerged."[2] In his autobiographical study of the Third Reich, Speer describes himself, using Ernst Cassirer's terms, as one of those "who of their own accord threw away man's highest privilege: to be an autonomous person."[3] But Speer's prominence in *The Führer Bunker* is attributable at least in part to his effort to recover this autonomy. Snodgrass credits him with "a real will" and points out that "he does have more will than almost any of the people in the poems, though he *seems* less willful" (I, p. 298). *The Führer Bunker*, as a whole, is a labyrinth of conflicting wills, assertive or abandoned within the orbit of that most willful and self-centered prisoner of his own delusions, Adolf Hitler.

This concern with autonomy is closely related to the other major theme of the cycle, the nature of betrayal. Questions of betrayal (and loyalty) are implicit in much of Snodgrass's early work, from the worried self-justification of "Heart's Needle: 3" ("Solomon himself might say / I am your real mother"), to the fierce, unwilling loyalty at the center of "A Flat One." But Hitler is for Snodgrass certainly the supreme study in betrayal. He is a man who set the pattern for his life by betraying his own stepbrother. Jealous of the older Alois, Hitler, with lies and his mother's connivance, was able to drive the boy away from home. According to Snodgrass, "being able to manipulate her to get what he wanted with regard to the stepbrother may have set the pattern that goes right through his life" (II, p. 404).

Speer is another kind of example. Snodgrass describes the paradox: "The media urge us to call him more moral. But he gave up his first ideals and took different ones. That made him a kind of betrayer to Göring. He did indeed seem like he was betraying them all" (II, p. 409). Göring, on the other hand, though "a dreadful man," may seem curiously more admirable precisely because he refuses, at the last, to change his mind or to evade responsibility. "What is betrayal and what isn't"—that, according to Snodgrass, is "a central theme" of the cycle.

This development of Snodgrass's concern with particular themes has a parallel in his increasing preference for multiple voices and diverse poetic forms as the means of their expression. We have already examined in detail how well tuned to specific concerns and occasions are the diverse poetic forms of "Heart's Needle," and we have followed the interplay of different voices in such later poems as "A Visitation" and "Manet: The Execution of the Emperor Maximilian." In *The Führer Bunker*, both of these principles seem to reach fruition: every speaker in the cycle becomes a complex and

autonomous character, and each, as Snodgrass says, "has a kind of
verse form that is typical of his or her personality."

Goebbels, for instance, speaks through couplets, many of which
seem to contain Pope's waspish humor and to reflect that
eighteenth-century poet's obsession with form. As we follow
Goebbels from poem to poem, he becomes, as Snodgrass points out,
"more and more vocally pinched." Varying enjambment and shifts
in tone prevent the Goebbels poems from becoming too patterned,
but the meanness of the man's mind as he approaches his end
becomes more and more clear.

Through the Hitler poems, Snodgrass seeks to convey "a mind
that was exceedingly brutal and powerful, but crude, really crude"
(I, p. 304). To convey this, he allows Hitler frequent ellipsis.
"Chunks of language" fall like blows of a hammer. What Snodgrass
calls "the civilized side of language," grammar and syntax, falls
away. Instead, Snodgrass allows to Hitler "the kind of simple,
brutal language which a child might have" (I, p. 304).

And in the Speer poems, form becomes almost hieroglyphic, a
kind of picture of the poem's content. Whatever the syntax,
whatever the logic, the lines in Speer's poems, stanza by stanza,
grow longer and longer until the stanza ends. On the simplest
dramatic level, the stanzas seem to form the steps that Speer must
use as he moves down toward and up away from Hitler during the
course of the poem. But more important, the continual lengthening
of the line, which begins to seem compulsive, can suggest the compulsion for growth that Speer shared with his Führer. When Speer
at one point is beset by frightening dreams and his attempts at self-
justification founder, the pattern changes: the stanza forms a compact square. The next stanza breaks down completely, and it is not
difficult to appreciate the significance of its collapse:

> What was it
> Hanke saw there in the camps?
> And warned me
> not to look?

This "kind of swimming form," as Snodgrass describes it, intimates
the disruptive force of Speer's conscience, now becoming restive
after years of inactivity. Then, when Speer lights a cigarette and
again takes control of his feelings, the triangles begin to form again,
though not at such ambitious length as before. Throughout the
poem, then, even the appearance of the stanzas is integral to their

developing a portrait of Speer's mind during the final days of the war.

The Magda Goebbels poems are perhaps an even more striking example of the use of form to convey information about a character that could not be effectively communicated otherwise. The villanelle form is so difficult—its form is rigidly prescribed and it allows only two rhymes throughout—that it easily can produce an impression of tension and repetitiousness. Thus Snodgrass found it ideal as a means of saying "things about her character that don't and perhaps couldn't get said in any other way" (II, p. 405). "The villanelle form," he explains, "helps give her the tightness I think she had" (II, p. 401).

Form becomes, in this case, means to a truer revelation of character. Her photographs make her appear genial enough, and she had a certain reputation, as Snodgrass remembers, for being "kind of loose and easy-going" (II, p. 401). But Snodgrass chose the villanelle form, and it seemed to lead him to recognition of the significance of her final action. "I could see her poems getting tighter and tighter, more tense and hate-filled and rigid. For a little while it worried me. I finally decided, no, that's right, she would have to have been that way or she couldn't have killed her six children" (II, pp. 401 - 402).

The narrative advantages of decorum, especially when there are so many radically different speakers in a work, are clearly substantial. As in the *Iliad,* when what a speaker says and the way he says it seem consistent with the particular character he reveals, we not only find that character the more credible, but we also become more sensitive to his conflicts with other characters.

In his experimentation with different forms and voices, however, Snodgrass is not seeking only such relatively obvious dividends. For one thing, his care in developing styles that convey the character of the speaker is as well a means of diminishing the presence of his own voice in the poem; he seeks to represent Hitler's voice, for instance, not to use the character of Hitler as a medium for his own. Further, multiple voices and styles enable a poet to get more of himself into a work. "You can't get the complete richness of your psyche into one poem," Snodgrass says. "So I guess one of the ways you try to do that is to write something like *The Führer Bunker,* where you have a whole lot of voices and hope to get in even more angles of yourself" (I, p. 299).

The most important motive behind Snodgrass's continuing experimentation with form and style, however, may rest on his conviction that the music of poetry—its rhythms, its sounds—can convey a substantial freight of meaning from the poet's unconscious to that of the reader. His interest in working with musical structures, as he once told Robert Boyers, is directly related to his wish "to get to something much more unconscious."[4] And, speaking of *The Führer Bunker*, Snodgrass has said, "I hope that the poem goes into areas I'm not conscious of at all. If the poem is going to last, it will have to" (II, p. 405).

By its attitudes, its concerns, and its exploitation of a rich variety of forms and styles, *The Führer Bunker* reveals itself as no radical aberration in Snodgrass's career, but the achievement of his steady growth. We have still to observe, though, what is perhaps the firmest link between "Heart's Needle" and *The Führer Bunker*, for it is one that depends on the combination of Snodgrass's distinctive attitudes, concerns, and stylistic virtuosity.

In our reading of "Heart's Needle," we developed an appreciation for "the depth of its sincerity," its honesty to the reality of the poet's thoughts and feelings. But in *The Führer Bunker*, the poet's thoughts and feelings are never explicit; were they to become so, the poem's dramatic integrity would be violated. Yet the "depth of sincerity" in this cycle about World War II is no less remarkable. It simply deserves a more fitting name: authenticity.

As in "Heart's Needle," the speakers in *The Führer Bunker* manage to persuade us of their reality. They assume distinct shapes in our minds and speak with candor and authority. The credibility of their statements may not be certain, for a man can misrepresent himself to himself, but the voices, the thoughts, convince.

Even more important, we find that as Snodgrass has conceived of his speakers according to his limited knowledge about them, he has insisted that his imagination be faithful to the ways in which he must conceive of them, rather than to ways in which he might prefer to conceive of them. Snodgrass's impression of the present day Speer as a likeable man has no discernible effect on the complex figure in the poem who shuttles to and from Hitler, "neglecting his knowing." Snodgrass's insight into the depths of Magda Goebbels' character developed as he worked on the villanelle. The Hitler of the cycle is remarkable for his weakness, his cruelty, and his self-delusion, but he is also, somehow, remarkable for his flawed humanity.

According to Snodgrass, the crucial questions about *The Führer Bunker* are these: Does it feel authentic? Does it feel like the way the world feels? These are also, and not by coincidence, the crucial questions about "Heart's Needle." To the extent that we can answer in the affirmative in both cases, we can appreciate the extent to which the Snodgrass of "Heart's Needle" has accomplished a bold new enterprise without surrendering the hard-won virtues of his earlier work.

II   *"Maybe one shouldn't write these poems"*

To the extent that history attempts not only to organize and record information, but also to report the experience of history, *The Führer Bunker* is a work of history as well as a cycle of poems. Snodgrass does not accept the contemporary split between history and poetry, anyway. "People who wrote the sagas thought they were writing history," he reminds us. And Snodgrass's cycle is indeed like a saga, in that he is at least as interested in present ways of perceiving the characters as he is in what they actually did. "In some way it may be true," he says, "that what we think those people did is truer than what they did" (I, p. 309).

A work of art built upon such a premise is, as we might expect, vulnerable to criticisms that have little to do with art. This is especially the case when the chosen subject is a highly sensitive one. The problem may be fortunate in the case of *The Führer Bunker*, however, for in Snodgrass's responses to actual or potential objections lie crucial revelations about what he intends in the work and about what he discovered in the process of creating it.

For instance, there is the danger that in any "authentic" first-person narrative, whether fiction or poetry, the mere presence of the speaker's voice may win him more sympathy than his actions deserve. After reading early versions of his *Bunker* poems, Snodgrass received a letter indicting him for "humanizing" the Nazis. Snodgrass's reply (never sent) isolates the kind of complacent moral superiority against which his poem is directed:

You can't blame *me* for humanizing the Nazis. God did that. They *were* human. If you desire to believe that they were *not* human, then you are guilty of exactly their worst crime, which is what they tried to do to the Jews, to believe that they were not human. . . .
What is involved here is one of the real, basic, terrible paradoxes of being alive, that your enemy *is* human and not so different from you. . . . To admit that you're not much better than the man you're killing is a pretty fearful thing. But there is a strong possibility that it is true. I suppose that is

one of the things the poem is trying to get at, ultimately. . . .

The aim of a work of art surely is to stretch the reader's psyche, to help him to identify with more people, with more life than he normally does. He is only going to be able to do that if you get him past his beliefs about right and wrong which keep him from seeing what ways in which he is like certain other people. . . . If the work of art *doesn't* bring the observer to see more of himself than he was aware of before, what use does it have to exist? (I, pp. 302 - 303)

Another charge, equally serious and perhaps equally misguided, might be that *The Führer Bunker* represents the fulfillment of the prophecy that it describes Goebbels as making: "They'll believe in us when we're dead"—that is, that the cycle of poems gives Goebbels and Hitler precisely the kind of eternal podium to which they aspired. Snodgrass's reply is conclusive.

My poems say much more awful things about the Nazis than their enemies ever said. Goebbels predicts that the Nazi philosophy will survive, that their mythology about themselves is what will survive. I hope that what I am getting here is not the mythologized Nazis at all, but the real ones. . . .

Their awful tendencies of personality have survived, indeed, as in our desire to believe that the Germans were not human, which seems to me just like their desire to believe the Jews not human. But Goebbels is predicting that their mythologized selves will survive. That isn't what I think. I think that, as a matter of fact, the realistic side of them is what has survived. (II, p. 407)

CHAPTER 8

The Promise of Maturity

AFTER the critical and popular success of *Heart's Needle* was no longer a matter for concern, Snodgrass became concerned instead about the dangers of success. He had perceived a disturbing phenomenon in twentieth-century American poetry: "We've had poet after poet with brilliant early poems, with a marvelous first book, sometimes with a marvelous two or three books, but none of the work in the middle age, the period we think of as maturity."[1] To Snodgrass at that time, the "essential case" seemed that of John Crowe Ransom, who stopped writing entirely in middle age after publishing brilliant collections as a young man. That Ransom eventually enjoyed "a very late flowering" made the silence of his middle age, of his maturity, seem even more ominous for Snodgrass.[2]

With his young man's success behind him, Snodgrass became fearful that his own career might repeat the process he had perceived in the careers of others. So he sought to try to understand the reasons behind the typical mid-career slump. Part of the explanation he found in his own experience. Early success, he discovered, frightens and inhibits the creative mind: "As soon as it becomes obvious to you that you could do some good work, and you receive recognition, you've got trouble . . . . All your deepest fears of your own energies get you."[3] This "trouble" leads in most cases, Snodgrass observed, to a retreat from the risks indigenous to continued growth as an artist. And such retreat takes the poet from feelings, his natural province, into ideas; afraid of their own powers, poets, by Snodgrass's view, too often "seem to turn into idea-mongers." The result? The typical American poet "simply doesn't have a mature period."[4]

Snodgrass's anxieties about his own maturity as a poet, which appear here in the form of historical hypotheses, provide an appropriate incentive for considering his relative significance at mid-career and for speculating briefly about his apparent potential, the promise of his lengthening career.

On the basis of *Heart's Needle* alone, we may describe Snodgrass as one of the most influential American poets of the century's third quarter. Robert Lowell and Anne Sexton are among those poets who have given Snodgrass just credit for initiating a rich and prominent if apparently short-lived strain in contemporary poetry—the "confessional" mode. Even more important for literary history, however, is Snodgrass's having defied, in his early work, the prevailing demands of New Criticism. His refusal to write the kind of poems that were being written at the time produced, as Lowell said, a clear breakthrough.

And on the basis of his subsequent work, we may count Snodgrass among the most ambitious and self-critical of his contemporaries. His career to date illustrates the well-known advice by Cocteau to young poets: "Learn what you can do and then don't do it." He writes comparatively little; yet what he does write, as we have seen, testifies to his continued willingness to take chances. He often succeeds, as the anthologists' tributes suggest, but his willingness to risk failure is a far more important indication of his continuing capacity for growth.

Yet, despite Snodgrass's acknowledged importance as an influence on modern poetry, despite the consistent excellence of his small oeuvre, and despite the artistic courage implicit in works such as *The Führer Bunker*, those who most admire Snodgrass want more. If Snodgrass is to emerge as one of the leading American poets of the century's final quarter, he must exploit more fully, more often, a talent that seems still as much potential as accomplished.

Those who seek encouragement that this development may take place may be able to find it, oddly enough, in two of Snodgrass's peripheral pursuits, his criticism and his translations. These endeavors, as much as the recent poems, reveal a poet intent on carefully establishing his creative priorities and perfecting his language. They are intrinsically interesting, informative, and often admirable. Yet the essays and translations seem as well the coherent exercises of a poet willing to forego the short gains of more frequent publication in reaching for those large, original, mature works that must be his alone.

The critical essays, on such writers as Dostoevsky, Shakespeare, Cervantes, Dante, and Homer, consistently reveal Snodgrass's eclectic reading, his skepticism regarding conventional literary judgments, and his poet's gift for pertinent and revealing associations. One reviewer of his collected critical essays, *In Radical Pursuit,* says: "What primarily distinguishes Snodgrass is the sheer originality of his thought; his essays are as full of surprises as his poems."[5] Like his poetry, Snodgrass's criticism gives the impression of a mind reaching beyond the pleasures of cleverness to the hard-won satisfactions of wisdom.

But Snodgrass's criticism may be related in an even more direct way to his poetry. For one thing, criticism provides the poet with an opportunity for direct expression of his ideas, thereby enabling him to give precedence in his poetry to other matters; good criticism may be at least in part a function of a disinclination for the poetry of ideas.

Snodgrass's essays do seem to bear such a relationship to his poems. As we read his study of the *Iliad,* we think of "Ten Days Leave" and Gardons' *Remains.* His study of *A Midsummer Night's Dream* raises issues of choice and emotional maturity dramatized in such poems as "Seeing You Have . . ." and "Home Town." The essay on *Crime and Punishment,* with its analysis of a protagonist who commits a crime in order to obtain the punishment he has always desired, should be required preparatory reading for *The Führer Bunker.* In short, the same ideas inform much of Snodgrass's poetry and criticism. Because these ideas receive coherent, logical development in the essays, they can work far beneath the surfaces of the poems.

It is likewise important that the essays provide the poet with the opportunity to develop, as well as to express, his ideas. In every one of his critical essays, Snodgrass must test his assumptions against the successful achievement of an independent work, an acknowledged masterpiece. One result is stronger ideas; though weak ideas may sometimes give rise to splendid poems, strong, coherent ideas seem to sustain the achievement of a mature body of work. We may perhaps assume that Snodgrass's work in criticism provides one source of the intellectual confidence that enables him to remain, in maturity, an active poet willing to take chances, to attempt a work big enough "so that if it is bad, it'll be *really* bad."[6]

Like his criticism, Snodgrass's translations constitute a diverse body of work, distinguished in its own right. As wide-ranging as the criticism, geographically and chronologically, the translations draw upon originals as different from one another as Rainer Maria Rilke's

Sonnets to Orpheus and the Romanian folk poem, *Mioritsa*. Victor Hugo and Rimbaud are among those who appear in translation in *After Experience*, and a collection of European troubadour songs appeared in the same year as *The Führer Bunker*.

In his translations, Snodgrass works from prose translations prepared by expert collaborators. Then, while holding as strictly as possible to the literal sense and word play of his original, he "tries to find his way out through the work, and tries to find a new way to orchestrate that work, using the instruments of the English language rather than [those of] the original."[7] The result, in many of Snodgrass's translations, is an effective English poem that may be closer in syntax to its original than a comparable "scholarly" version.[8]

For the admirer of Snodgrass's original poetry, though, the translations have an importance that goes beyond their intrinsic merits. First, Snodgrass's early translations provided him with the opportunity to experiment with the simple, straightforward style that he would later adopt for the poems of *Heart's Needle*. That Randall Jarrell preferred Snodgrass's translations of Rilke to his "imitation Lowell" urged Snodgrass toward the style that proved essential not only to *Heart's Needle*, but also to Gardons' *Remains* and to much of *After Experience*.[9]

Second, by Snodgrass's own account, translations have provided him with a continuing creative outlet at times when the pressures of writing poems demanding his deep personal involvement have grown unbearable. "There are times when your own work is just too painful to face," Snodgrass has said. "Yet you want to keep your hand in, you want to do something."[10] There are only two other alternatives, both amply illustrated by the record of contemporary American poetry. One is artistic and emotional exhaustion. The other is silence. In turning often to his translations, Snodgrass has chosen the better way.

Third, Snodgrass's work with translations, by exposing him to a rich diversity of poetic (and musical) ends and means, has encouraged the increasing linguistic, metrical, and structural diversity of his own work. His attempt to develop in *The Führer Bunker* a compendium of verse forms and competing voices clearly owes something to the wide experience he has obtained in working through the forms and voices of other writers. Moreover, deep personal engagement with the works of other writers should weigh against a poet's lapsing, in the maturity of his career, into safe self-repetition; he remains (or should) too much aware of how many other possibilities there are.

Finally, translation has given Snodgrass the opportunity of experiencing to a singular extent the capacity of art to attack "the reader's narrow definitions of himself and what he believes and what he thinks."[11] This premise, as we have seen, underlies *The Führer Bunker*. But Snodgrass has placed himself on the receiving end as well. Effective translation, he has said, "amounts to entering into another man's psyche."[12] And when he decided to translate, for instance, Rilke's *Sonnets to Orpheus*, he set himself the task of "finding his way out" through poems that seem the product of a talent far different in nature from his own. Rilke believed his poems had been "given" to him, dictated by an outside voice. Rilke went so far as to contend that he understood his own *Sonnets to Orpheus* only imperfectly at first, that he required moments of grace in later life to grow into a fuller understanding of them.[13] The artistic assumptions at work in such a cycle are rather different, we may think, from those of a poet who insists: "No voices talk to me. If there *are* any voices, they're not speaking to me. I've never had such an experience."[14] Such willingness on Snodgrass's part to submit himself in the most thoroughgoing way possible to the aggression of poets different in important ways from himself seems a further measure of his philosophical and artistic commitment to relativism and, thus, a further means of defense against a maturity of weary ideamongering.

But such conjectures cannot take us finally very far into the future. If Snodgress achieves the fruitful maturity of which he seems capable, he may well find himself among the most powerful of late twentieth-century voices. But all that is certain is that the conditions for his continued growth as a poet seem good and that those who have admired Snodgrass in the past have ample reason to be optimistic about his future. At the very least (if I may use Snodgrass's description of Dante), this poet who has moved from poems about his daughter to poems about paintings to poems about Hitler seems committed to "a life not of containment and stasis, but of movement and change."[15]

Notes and References

Chapter One

1. "Finding a Poem" (1959), *In Radical Pursuit* (New York: Harper & Row, 1975), p. 32.
2. Robert Boyers, "W. D. Snodgrass: An Interview," *Salmagundi*, Nos. 22 - 23 (Spring-Summer 1973), p. 151.
3. "An Elm Tree," *Counter Measures*, 1 (1972), 13.
4. "Cherry Saplings," *Salmagundi*, Nos. 22 - 23 (Spring-Summer 1973), p. 16.
5. Suzanne Henig, "Conversation with John Lehmann," *Journal of Modern Literature*, 3 (February 1973), 92. Snodgrass himself once said, "I don't think I was doing anything different from what poets have always done." See David Dillon, " 'Toward Passionate Utterance': An Interview with W. D. Snodgrass," *Southwest Review*, 60 (Summer 1975), 279.
6. Jerome—Mazzaro, "Public Intimacy," *The Nation*, 207 (September 16, 1968), 253.
7. William Heyen, "Fishing the Swamp: The Poetry of W. D. Snodgrass," in *Modern American Poetry: Essays in Criticism*, ed. Jerome Mazzaro (New York: David McKay, 1970), p. 361.
8. M. L. Rosenthal, *The New Poets* (New York: Oxford University Press, 1967), p. 67.
9. " 'No Voices Talk to Me': A Conversation with W. D. Snodgrass," ed. Philip L. Gerber and Robert J. Gemmett, *Western Humanities Review*, 24 (Winter 1970), 67.
10. Rosenthal, p. 67.
11. "A Poem's Becoming" (1960), *In Radical Pursuit*, p. 53.
12. Judson Jerome, "Poets of the Sixties," *Antioch Review*, 19 (Fall 1959), 422.
13. Quoted in *Contemporary Poets of the English Language*, ed. Rosalie Murphy (New York: St. Martin's Press, 1970), p. 1024.
14. Paul Carroll, *The Poem in Its Skin* (Chicago: Follett, 1968), p. 175.
15. M. L. Rosenthal, "Notes from the Future: Two Poets," *The Nation*, 189 (October 24, 1959), 257.
16. X. J. Kennedy, *An Introduction to Poetry*, 2nd ed. (Boston: Little, Brown and Co., 1971), p. 11.
17. Gerber and Gemmett, p. 62.
18. Mazzaro, "Public Intimacy," p. 252.
19. Rosenthal, "Notes," p. 257.

20. Gerber and Gemmett, p. 70.

21. Donald T. Torchiana, "*Heart's Needle*: Snodgrass Strides Through the Universe," *Tri-Quarterly*, 2 (Spring 1960), 20.

22. Snodgrass's most thorough description of this process is in a letter to J. D. McClatchy. See "W. D. Snodgrass: The Mild, Reflective Art," *The Massachusetts Review*, 16 (Spring 1975), 286 - 87.

23. "Finding a Poem," p. 32.

24. "Poems About Paintings," *In Radical Pursuit*, p. 66.

25. Boyers, *Salmagundi*, p. 161.

26. "Preface," *In Radical Pursuit*, p. xii.

Chapter Two

1. McClatchy, pp. 286 - 87.

2. McClatchy, p. 286.

3. "This future would conform to an image or Dasein which is shaped coevally with a will to exist and which is so generally valid that it would allow one's ability to choose to become a decision for the whole of mankind." Mazzaro, "The Public Intimacy of W. D. Snodgrass" [revised and enlarged version of "Public Intimacy"], *Salmagundi*, No. 19 (Spring 1972), p. 100.

4. A subjective, provocative analysis of principles of organization in "At the Park Dance" appears in Richard Howard, *Alone With America* (New York: Atheneum, 1969), pp. 474 - 75.

5. Snodgrass's opinion is well-balanced. "There are a good many poems that I couldn't begin to understand, if I didn't know something about their authors," he says. But in commenting on the freight of private experiences borne by his own poem, "These Trees Stand . . .," he says, "I don't know how much a person has to know about these things to understand it" (Gerber and Gemmett, pp. 62 - 63).

6. Robert Phillips, *The Confessional Poets* (Carbondale and Edwardsville: Southern Illinois University Press, 1973), p. 51.

7. Many such local references are identified in Torchiana, pp. 18 - 26.

8. Pierrot, with a white face and white clothes, is a stock figure in classical pantomime. The English apply the name to clowns who affect a similar appearance.

9. Phillips, pp. 52 - 53.

10. "Preface," *In Radical Pursuit*, p. xii.

11. "Tact and the Poet's Force," *In Radical Pursuit*, p. 8.

12. "Moonshine and Sunny Beams," *In Radical Pursuit*, p. 212.

13. "A Poem's Becoming," p. 42.

14. McClatchy, p. 292.

15. "A Poem's Becoming," p. 42.

16. *Ibid*.

17. Torchiana, p. 22.

18. Gerber and Gemmett, p. 62.

19. *Ibid.*

20. *Ibid.*

21. Jerome, p. 430.

22. Torchiana, p. 22.

23. Carroll, p. 182.

24. Karl Malkoff, "W. D. Snodgrass," in *Crowell's Handbook of Contemporary American Poetry* (New York: Crowell, 1973), p. 299.

25. Torchiana (p. 22) provides many such details. He mentions Snodgrass's "trips to the university dental clinic," names the Mahler song "taught to one Rachel Chester, a most promising young painter," says that the "lessons in moth lore and affection" were "for Jan's daughter by an earlier marriage," and identifies the "old man who was dying" as Fritz Jarck, "whom Snodgrass tended in the hospital." For a brief discussion of the disagreement on the "song of Mahler's," see McClatchy, pp. 295n - 96n.

26. Jerome, p. 430.

Chapter Three

1. Boyers, p. 151.

2. Torchiana, p. 20.

3. Boyers, p. 163.

4. Lowell's comment is printed on the dustjacket of *Heart's Needle.*

5. Boyers, p. 152; in a letter to McClatchy, Snodgrass says, "I think my chief influences were musical" (McClatchy, p. 285n).

6. McClatchy, pp. 283 - 84.

7. This information and the quotation are in a letter from Snodgrass to McClatchy, p. 283n.

8. "Finding a Poem," p. 283.

9. Boyers, p. 163.

10. "Finding a Poem," p. 283.

11. *Ibid.*

12. Mazzaro notes that Lowell gave credit to "Heart's Needle" as an influence on *Life Studies* (Mazzaro, "The Public Intimacy," p. 104). And Malkoff (p. 299) reports that "Anne Sexton once remarked that it was not Robert Lowell but W. D. Snodgrass who first opened up for her the possibilities of a searingly personal kind of poetry. . . ."

13. Also from the dustjacket comment.

14. Hayden Carruth, "Three Poets," *Poetry*, 95 (November 1959), 120 - 21.

15. Jerome, p. 429.

16. Donald Hall, "True Feeling and Good Eyes," New York *Herald-Tribune Book Review*, July 19, 1959, p. 3.

17. William Dickey, "W. D. Snodgrass, *Heart's Needle*," *Epoch*, 9 (Spring 1959), 256.

18. The seasonal references, along with titles, appear over the poems in a

typescript held in the Theodore Roethke Collection by the Suzzallo Library of the University of Washington. See McClatchy, pp. 296 - 97n. All future references to titling of the poems in "Heart's Needle" draw on McClatchy's information.

19. Hall, p. 3.

20. David Farrelly, "Heart's Fling: The Poetry of W. D. Snodgrass," *Perspective*, 13 (Winter 1964), 189.

21. Boyers, p. 161.

22. Dickey, pp. 254 - 55.

23. Phillips, pp. 45 - 72.

24. Howard, p. 478.

25. "Finding a Poem," p. 283.

26. McClatchy, p. 297.

27. "Finding a Poem," p. 283.

28. Farrelly (p. 193) calls the poem a "prologue." According to Snodgrass (*Heart's Needle*, p. 41), the title phrase is taken from "an Old Irish story, The Frenzy of Suibne, as translated by Myles Dillon."

29. Dante Alighieri, *The Divine Comedy: Paradiso*, tr. Charles S. Singleton, Bollingen Series 80 (Princeton: Princeton University Press, 1975), pp. 33, 31.

30. Boyers, p. 157.

31. Phillips, p. 59.

32. "Finding a Poem," p. 24.

33. *Ibid.*, pp. 26 - 27.

34. *Ibid.*, p. 28. The original version of the essay (*Partisan Review*, 26 [Spring 1959], 276 - 83) contains a harsher and more detailed conjecture regarding the death.

35. *Ibid.*, p. 28.

36. *Ibid.*, p. 32.

37. *Ibid.*, p. 24.

38. See Farrelly, p. 197; biblical references are Ezekiel 14: 13 - 20, 18: 1 - 32; Jeremiah 31: 29 - 30.

39. The typescript in the Roethke collection bears the title "Deadlock."

40. The phrase is that of William Heyen, p. 361.

Chapter Four

1. "Finding A Poem," pp. 23 - 32.

2. *Ibid.*, p. 28.

Chapter Five

1. Heyen, p. 352.

2. Jim Harrison, "Fresh Usual Words," *New York Times Book Review*, April 28, 1968, p. 6.

3. Howard, p. 480.

4. Personal interview with Snodgrass, January 2, 1977.
5. Heyen, p. 361.
6. McClatchy, p. 309.
7. *Ibid.*, p. 310.
8. Phillips, p. 68.
9. See Paul L. Gaston, "W. D. Snodgrass and *The Führer Bunker:* An Interview," *Papers on Language and Literature,* 13 (Summer 1977), 301.
10. *Ibid.*, p. 303.
11. *Ibid.*, pp. 302 - 303.
12. *Ibid.*
13. Baruch Spinoza, *Ethics* and *On the Correction of the Understanding,* tr. Andrew Boyle (New York: Dutton, 1959), p. 227.
14. *Ibid.*, p. 231.

Chapter Six

1. Snodgrass's essay, "Poems About Paintings" (*In Radical Pursuit,* pp. 63 - 97), is a thorough discussion of his intentions in these poems and of the steps he followed in developing them, but its main points stimulate rather than impede further inquiry. Further references appear in the text, preceded by the abbreviation *RP.*
2. Howard, p. 483.
3. Mazzaro, "The Public Intimacy," p. 105.
4. "Preface to the Tokyo Exhibition," *Matisse on Art,* ed. and trans. Jack D. Flam (New York: Phaidon, 1973), p. 127.
5. Jean Guichard-Meili, *Matisse* (New York: Praeger, 1967), p. 210.
6. Snodgrass's assumption that critics typically regard Vuillard as an essentially decorative painter is not suggested by recent art criticism. Jacques Salomon's comment that Vuillard "discreetly initiates us into the mystery of these silent, modest rooms where he spent his youth" suggests Snodgrass's interpretation, as does John Russell's view that Vuillard, despite his faithfulness to the bourgeoisie, clearly does not represent "compromise and acquiescence" to such conditions of this life as "apartness made visible." Salomon, *Vuillard* (Paris: La Bibliotheque des Arts, p. 9 [translation mine]; Russell, "Vuillard, or the Discreet Charm of the Bourgeoisie," *Artnews,* 72 (March 1973), 25.
7. William Seitz, *Claude Monet: Seasons and Moments* (New York: The Museum of Modern Art, 1960), pp. 51 - 52.
8. *Ibid.*
9. As Robert Rey once pointed out, Manet's emphasis on the dress and posture of the firing squad "reduces the aspect of this tragic moment to that of some firing exercise on the parade ground." *Manet,* tr. Eveline Byam Shaw (Paris: Hyperion Press, 1938), p. 14.
10. Georges Bataille, *Manet,* tr. Austryn Wainhouse and James Emmons (New York: Skira, n.d.), pp. 51 - 52.

11. George Heard Hamilton, *Manet and His Critics* (New Haven: Yale University Press, 1954), p. 278.

12. Rey, p. 14.

Chapter Seven

1. References in the text are to Paul L. Gaston, "W. D. Snodgrass and *The Führer Bunker:* An Interview," *Papers on Language and Literature,* 13 (Summer 1977), 295 - 311 [I], and 13 (Fall 1977), 401 - 412 [II].

2. H. R. Trevor-Roper, *The Last Days of Hitler* (New York: Macmillan, 1947), p. 241.

3. Albert Speer, *Inside the Third Reich* (New York: Macmillan, 1970), p. 49.

4. Boyers, p. 156.

Chapter Eight

1. "Poetry Since Yeats: An Exchange of Views," *Tri-Quarterly,* No. 9 (Spring 1967), p. 101.

2. *Ibid.*

3. Boyers, p. 160.

4. *Ibid.,* p. 161.

5. Richard Horwich, "Critical Feast," *The New Republic,* February 15, 1975, p. 31.

6. Gaston, I, p. 307.

7. Gerber and Gemmett, p. 68.

8. E.g., compare Snodgrass's translation of the simple "Galgenkindes Wiegenlied" (Christian Morgenstern, *Gallows Songs,* tr. W. D. Snodgrass and Lore Segal [Ann Arbor: University of Michigan Press, 1967], no. 55) with that of the respected Max Knight (Berkeley: University of California Press, 1964), p. 52.

9. McClatchy, pp. 283 - 84.

10. Gerber and Gemmett, p. 68.

11. Gaston, I, p. 303.

12. Gerber and Gemmett, p. 68.

13. Idris Parry, "Rilke and Orpheus," (London) *Times Literary Supplement,* No. 3848 (December 12, 1975), p. 1494.

14. Gerber and Gemmett, p. 71.

15. "Analysis of Depths: The *Inferno,*" *In Radical Pursuit,* p. 318.

Selected Bibliography

PRIMARY SOURCES

After Experience. New York: Harper & Row, 1968.
The Führer Bunker. Brockport, New York: BOA Editions, 1977.
Gallows Songs. By Christian Morgenstern. Tr. with Lore Segal. Ann Arbor: University of Michigan Press, 1967.
Heart's Needle. New York: Alfred A. Knopf, 1959; Hessle, England: The Marvell Press, 1960.
In Radical Pursuit [Essays]. New York: Harper & Row, 1975.
Six Troubadour Songs [Translations with music]. Providence, Rhode Island: Burning Deck, 1977.
Traditional Hungarian Songs [Translations with music]. Baltimore: Charles Seluzicki at The Janus Press, 1978.
(For reasons explained in the text, S. S. Gardons' *Remains* [Mt. Horeb, Wisconsin: The Perishable Press, 1970] must be considered a "primary source" for the study of Snodgrass.)

(Uncollected Original Poems)

"Cherry Saplings." *Salmagundi,* Nos. 22 - 23 (Spring-Summer 1973), p. 16.
"Coming Down From the Acropolis." *Agenda,* Nos. 12 - 13 (Winter-Spring 1975), pp. 50 - 51.
"An Elm Tree." *Counter Measures,* 1 (1972), 13.
"Good Friday." *Western Review,* 15 (Summer 1951), 268.
" 'The Last Toot' from *What Ever Happened to Father?*" *Experiment,* 6 (1951), 9. [The projected cycle from which this poem seems to have been excerpted was not written.]
"Letter." *Transatlantic Review,* No. 1 (Summer 1959), p. 32. [Included in British edition of *Heart's Needle.*]
"Old Apple Trees." *New Yorker,* May 1, 1971, p. 41; *Agenda,* 11 (1973), 71 - 72.
"Owls." *Counter Measures,* 1 (1972), 12; *Agenda,* 11 (1973), 70.
"A Phoebe's Nest." *Salmagundi,* Nos. 22 - 23 (Spring-Summer 1973), p. 17.
"The Sealchie's Son." *Agenda,* Nos. 12 - 13 (Winter-Spring 1975), 51 - 52.
"Seasoning Barn." *Salmagundi,* Nos. 22 - 23 (Spring-Summer 1973), p. 19.
"Setting Out." *Agenda,* Nos. 12 - 13 (Winter-Spring 1975), pp. 51 - 52; *University of Windsor Review,* 11 (Spring 1976), 58 - 59.
"Window Shopping." *Epoch,* 7 (Fall 1956), 223.

(Uncollected Translations)

"Autumn." [Trans. with Tanya Tolstoy from "originals" by the Russian "poet," Kozma Petrovich Prutkov, who was invented as a hoax by several Russian youths. Among them was Count Alexey Tolstoy, a distant ancestor of Miss Tolstoy.] *TriQuarterly*, No. 1 (Fall 1964), p. 33.

"Dalea-Damean and Sila." [Romanian ballad.] *Romanian Bulletin*, 6 (June 1977), pp. 6 - 7, 12. Also in *Miorita*, 5 (January 1978), 88 - 91.

"Epitaphs from Sapinta." [Twenty epitaphs from grave markers in a Romanian cemetery.] In *Romanian Folk Arts* [Proceedings of a symposium held at Duquesne University, November 8 - 9, 1974]. New York: The Romanian Library, n.d. Pp. 49 - 53.

"In Praise of Reason." [Trans. of "Lob des Hohen Verstands" from Gustav Mahler's *Des Knaben Wunderhorn*.] *Quarterly Review of Literature*, 10 (1960), 140 - 41.

"The Lady and the Tarantula: A Fable." [Trans. with Tanya Tolstoy from Prutkov "original."] *TriQuarterly*, No. 1 (Fall 1964), p. 33.

"Mesterul Manole" ("Master Builder Manole"). [Romanian ballad.] *Romanian Bulletin*, 5 (September 1976) 6 - 8.

"Miorita" ("Ewe Lamb"). [Trans. of Romanian ballad with Simone Draghici and Ioan Popa.] *Agenda*, 12 (Autumn 1974), 64 - 67. Also in *Romanian Folk Arts*. New York: The Romanian Library, n.d. Pp. 47 - 48. Also in limited Romanian editions. Also in *American Fabrics / Fashions* No. 109 (Spring 1977), pp. xvi.

"Poems in the Style of Heine." [Trans. with Tanya Tolstoy from Prutkov "originals." Incl. "I: With Sarcastic Overtones," "II: With Ironic Overtones," and "III: Ordinary."] *North American Review*, N.S. 1 (Summer 1964), 49.

"Six Romanian Folk Songs." *Odyssey*, 2 (November 1977), 9 - 10.

"Somnoroase Pasarele" ("Now the Song Birds"). [Trans. with N. Babuts of work by Romanian poet, Mihai Eminescu.] *Editiuns Della Revista Rotoromontcha a cura de Augustin Maissen:* Seminar in Romance Languages, the University of North Carolina. Chapel Hill, 1975. N.p. Also in *Romanian Bulletin*, 6 (January 1976), 6 - 7. Also in Marotta, Tom. *For They Are All My Friends* [photographs.] New York: Art reflections, 1977. N.p.

"Soarele si Luna" ("The Sun and the Moon"). [Romanian Ballad.] *Romanian Bulletin*, 6 (October 1977), 6 - 7.

"Three Minnesinger Pieces." [Incl. "Es Fuegt Sich," by Oswald von Wolkenstein; "Hie vor Do Wir Kinder Wären," by Meister Alexander; and "Unter der Linden," by Walter von der Vogelweide.] *Maryland Poetry Review*, 1 (1973), pp. 34 - 40.

"Three Traditional Ballads." [Incl. "Mass for the Dead" (German), "The Baron's Daughter" (Hungarian), and "The White Doe" (French).] *Counter Measures*, 3 (1974), 36 - 42.

"Versions of Kozma Prutkov." [Trans. with Tanya Tolstoy from Prutkov "originals." Incl. "Love of Honor," "The Heron and the Racing Rig," "Romanza," "A Poet's Will," "Rememberance of Things Past," "Junker Schmidt," "The Worm and the Deaconess," "Forget-Me-

Nots and Footboards," and "My Portrait."] *Poetry,* 104 (July 1964), 203 - 209.
"You, the Heaven's Domed Height." [Trans. of song by Bálint Balassi.] *The New Hungarian Quarterly,* 11 (Summer 1970), 65.

SECONDARY SOURCES

BOYERS, ROBERT. "W. D. Snodgrass: An Interview." *Salmagundi,* Nos. 22 - 23 (Spring-Summer 1973), pp. 149 - 63. Many of Boyers' questions are ones often put to Snodgrass, but Snodgrass does develop a lengthy statement on the problems American poets have had with maturity.
CARROLL, PAUL. *The Poem in Its Skin.* Chicago: Follett, 1968. Pp. 171 - 87. Largely unsympathetic but provocative criticism of *Heart's Needle.*
DILLON, DAVID. " 'Toward Passionate Utterance': An Interview with W. D. Snodgrass." *Southwest Review,* 60 (Summer 1975), 278 - 95. The discussion of translation and of the poems on paintings provides some new information.
FARRELLY, DAVID. "Heart's Fling: The Poetry of W. D. Snodgrass." *Perspective,* 13 (Winter 1964), 185 - 99. Graceful close readings of the best-known poems in *Heart's Needle* supply many informative details. Emphasis is on the title sequence.
GASTON, PAUL L. "W. D. Snodgrass and *The Führer Bunker:* An Interview." *Papers on Language and Literature,* 13 (Summer 1977), 295 - 311; and 13 (Fall 1977), 401 - 12. Snodgrass discusses the assumptions and intentions behind his most recent poetry.
GERBER, PHILIP L., and ROBERT J. GEMMETT, eds. " 'No Voices Talk to Me': A Conversation with W. D. Snodgrass." *Western Humanities Review,* 24 (Winter 1970), 61 - 71. A thorough, well-edited interview in which Snodgrass discusses his criticism and translations as well as his early poetry.
HEYEN, WILLIAM. "Fishing the Swamp: The Poetry of W. D. Snodgrass." In *Modern American Poetry: Essays in Criticism,* ed. Jerome Mazzaro, pp. 351 - 68. New York: David McKay Co., 1970. Effectively distinguishes the early Snodgrass from other "autobiographical" poets and suggests useful comparisons between *Heart's Needle* and *After Experience.*
HOWARD, RICHARD. *Alone With America.* New York: Atheneum, 1969. Pp. 471 - 84. Highly sensitive to patterns in Snodgrass's biography and early poetry, this study provides superb explications of such poems as "At the Park Dance." These are far more helpful than some of its psychological and biographical conjectures.
MCCLATCHY, J. D. "W. D. Snodgrass: The Mild, Reflective Art." *The Massachusetts Review,* 16 (Spring 1975), 281 - 314. The most articulate appreciation of Snodgrass's "confessional mode," this study also provides much new biographical and critical information.

McClatchy deftly builds upon previous criticism as he develops fresh, comprehensive perspectives on Snodgrass's major work.

MAZZARO, JEROME. "The Public Intimacy of W. D. Snodgrass." *Salmagundi*, No. 19 (Spring 1972), pp. 96 - 111. Persuasive explications in this study of *Heart's Needle* and *After Experience* support its interest in Snodgrass's "ability to work positively" on his readers, "not by moral but by precept."

PHILLIPS, ROBERT. *The Confessional Poets*. Carbondale and Edwardsville: Southern Illinois University Press, 1973. Pp. 45 - 72. Analysis of *Heart's Needle* is so perceptive and generous that the too easy dismissal of *After Experience* is startling. Phillips pays special attention to the music and imagery of the early poems.

ROSENTHAL, M. L. *The New Poets*. New York: Oxford University Press, 1967. Inexplicably, Rosenthal gives little space to Snodgrass, but his book is required for study of any contemporary American poet.

SEULEAN, IOAN. "Romanian Ballads Translated into English." *Romanian Bulletin*, 7 (January 1978), 11 - 12. A native speaker's assessment of Snodgrass's Romanian translations.

TORCHIANA, DONALD T. "*Heart's Needle:* Snodgrass Strides Through the Universe." *Tri-Quarterly*, 2 (Spring 1960), 18 - 26. An engaging chronicle by an appreciative, sensitive reader who was one of Snodgrass's colleagues at Iowa. Solid explications coexist with informal, revealing anecdotes about life in and around the poetry workshop.

WHITE, WILLIAM. *W. D. Snodgrass: A Bibliography*. Detroit: Wayne State University Library, 1960. A meticulous record of publications by and about Snodgrass through 1960. Includes detailed bibliographical descriptions of early printings in the first edition of *Heart's Needle*. White is now preparing a current and comprehensive bibliography, which should be the definitive bibliographical resource for students of Snodgrass's work.

Index

171